REWRITE THE RULES

REWRITE
THE
RULES

An Unconventional Way
to Build an Intentional Life

ALEX ⚒ STARR

WINDGRAVE
—PUBLISHING—

Editor: Greg Larson
Book Launch Manager: Jesse Sussman
Cover Designer: Cindy Curtis
Printed in the United States of America

Windgrave Publishing and Rewrite the Rules
are registered trademarks of Windgrave LLC

windgravepublishing.com

REWRITE THE RULES

An Unconventional Way to Build an Intentional Life

ISBN 978-1-7359980-0-8 (paperback)
ISBN 978-1-7359980-1-5 (ebook)

To my parents

For showing what it means to provide,
to push forward and to love.

Contents

"I don't really want to become normal, average, standard. I want merely to gain in strength, in the courage to live out my life more fully, enjoy more, experience more. I want to develop even more original and more unconventional traits."

—Anais Nin

Introduction

BURN OFF THE DEAD WOOD

You are special. It's true what they say: every person is a unique entity with a soul and spirit that is vast with potential and possibilities. There will never be another person like you on Earth.

All of your experiences, setbacks, dreams, pains, and thoughts are 100 percent yours and yours alone. You are an energetic, conscious being that is aware of itself to a degree unfathomable to other species on the same planet. You have been blessed with life.

You are also nothing at all.

You couldn't be further from unique or special because we are *all* unique and special. You are a speck of matter on a giant rock that's revolving around a star in one solar system of millions within a billion galaxies that comprise an ever-expanding universe. People have come before you and many people will come after you. Most likely, after about 100 years, nobody will remember that you existed at all.

It's from this vast understanding that our lives take shape.

Sometimes, the weight of what you think you're supposed to do with that life feels overwhelming. The anxiety of not knowing is even worse.

That weight keeps you from doing what you were *born* to do. You're like a forest, suffocated by the accumulating dead wood of everyone else's expectations.

The dead wood builds and builds, causing us to desperately try to find something that makes sense, that pulls everything together, finally, and lets us relax, knowing *exactly* where we want to go and who we want to be for the next decade of our lives.

That's what happened to me when I graduated high school. My parents, teachers, counselors—it felt like everyone and their damn mailman was asking me the same thing:

"What are you going to do with your life, Alex?"

I shrugged my shoulders and muttered something about college, but I didn't know what I wanted to do any more than you do. I only knew what I *didn't* want to do.

I didn't want an office job, or some other 9-5.

I didn't want to live a life of regret.

And I didn't want to feel stuck in life.

So I joined a domestic version of the Peace Corps called "AmeriCorps" straight out of college. We helped at homeless shelters in the middle of a Colorado winter, built trails on ranches deep in the heart of Texas, and I met more interesting people than I can hope to remember.

The path started to form in front of my eyes, a different

route than what I was constantly being reminded of having left behind. The path led me into becoming a Wildland Firefighter, stationed in southern Arizona.

It was an exhilarating position that allowed me to make some money and travel in the offseason (yeah, firefighting has seasons the same way football or basketball does). It sounds like a badass profession. It ticked off enough of my "things I don't want to do" boxes that I stuck with it for four years. But still…it wasn't enough.

Because running away from what you don't want can only get you so far. Eventually, you have to run toward something you *do* want. But you can't do that until you know what it is.

Finally Leave the Hometown of Your Mind

Why does it feel so easy to slip and get lost along the way? Maybe because we were never meant to be on this specific path at all. "Progress" in a certain direction doesn't always mean going up. We've all been born at this particular time in history in this particular place— wherever that may be for you. You didn't choose it. We inherited the system, the structure of what is what and who is who.

The hierarchy. The learning. The government. What jobs look like. What a relationship looks like. How to eat and what to eat. The types of clothing we have and the words that spill out of our mouths.

Everything has been influenced by the place you were born and the era in which we have all come into being. I'm not suggesting that this is a bad thing. I'm not really suggesting it's a good thing either. But it's there, an itch that's hard to scratch. Where does it all lead and why?

As a podcast host for over five years, I've talked to and worked with Navy SEALs, polyamorous lovers, CEOs, world travelers, former gang members, entrepreneurs, and a particularly insightful guy who has essentially given up money. At some point, even when they've had everything they thought they wanted, they felt a lack. In some sense, everyone is still stuck in the hometown of their mind.

So if you picked up this book because you don't know where you're going in life, and the standard "rules" of engagement—get good grades, go to college, get a soulless job, marry someone you barely like, retire at 65 and enjoy life then—don't work for you, then I have one word for you: welcome.

Take a seat and get comfortable because I've been there before (and, depending on the day of the week, still frequently find myself there). I want to give you a simple framework to help you get through the struggles you're facing right now.

What you'll get out of this book is the beacon of possibility and some of the ways to start down the path… whether that's now, in 2 weeks, or 20 years.

Doing this takes courage, but not in a crazy way. Sometimes it just takes realizing that we can do more than we thought. Sometimes it's admitting that we can't do as much as we had hoped. And sometimes it's about re-evaluating where the compass is pointing in the first place.

You Are Already Everything You Seek

I have some bad news: you will never, ever, *ever* feel like you have it all figured out. Let that notion go right now. The race will never finish. You can walk across the most beautiful springtime valleys, surrounded by snowcapped mountains and refreshing glacial lakes with your lover, and if you're being honest with yourself, you'll still feel like there's something missing.

That's the secret that nobody wants to tell you—not the gurus, your parents, the government, especially any advertiser: no matter what you do, who you're with, or what you get, it will never feel like enough. Everyone perpetuates the illusion that once you get what you want (or what you think you want), you will feel complete. I'll let Thich Nhat Hanh, a Vietnamese monk, explain the actual truth of the matter for me:

> "You already are everything you are seeking. Do not try to become something else. The flower does not try to become the sun; it already is the sun. When you achieve this insight, you stop suffering. We suffer because we want to deny ourselves. We want to become something else, and so we never stop running."

I get it. What I'm telling you seems hopeless. If striving for something more is futile, why strive at all? That's a fair question, and I've definitely asked that of myself many times. But that's a shallow response to a deep conundrum.

I didn't write this book to convince you that all effort and achievement is meaningless. Just the opposite. I wrote this book to show you how to get where you want to be—to rewrite the rules according to your own desires, not society's—knowing full well that whatever you achieve will be more for the journey than the destination.

You'll like where you go. But if you don't enjoy the going part, you'll miss out on the marrow of life.

Up in Smoke

Using examples from my life and the countless people I've spoken to and worked with, this book will show you how to peer around the corner to answer these questions from where you are, to get closer to where you want to be. I'm not talking about saying "fuck you" to every establishment and tradition and start living in the back of a dirty van eating only vegan pancakes and moaning over the full moon's energetic chakra.

Not at all.

I'm suggesting that you become aware of it and change your perception from within. That's what this book aims to help you do.

This is for *you* who's wondering, "What's next?" or

"How do I reconnect with my place in all of this?" I want to help you because I've been you—I *am* you.

Everyone else's expectations and rules are like dead wood accumulating on the forest floor of your life. And if there's one thing I learned in firefighting, it's that dead wood needs to be burned off before it incinerates the entire forest.

Are you ready to burn off the unnecessary rules that have been dictated to you and rewrite those rules according to your standards, your beliefs, and your goals?

After you set all that dead wood ablaze, the strongest trees of who you actually are will remain.

Time to let it burn.

CHAPTER 1

What the Hell Are Pickle Seeds?

I flipped through every seed packet in the hardware store. They had it all: tomato seeds, carrot seeds, pepper seeds, flower seeds, and everything in between. Everything except the only seeds I needed.

"Damn," I thought. "No pickle seeds."

I walked up to the old man working the register and told him my predicament. "Where are the pickle seeds?" I asked.

He looked at me and smiled in amusement. "You can buy cucumber seeds," he said, then pointed to the canned goods in the back, "or you can buy pickles in a jar. But we don't sell pickle seeds. Nobody in the world does, I'm afraid."

Was this dude messing with me? "I don't want cucumbers, or pre-canned pickles. I just want to grow the pickles myself."

"I'm not sure what you're asking for. You can buy cucumbers and pickle them. You can grow zucchinis or carrots and pickle them. But you can't buy pickle seeds. Things *get* pickled after they've grown."

The room started to spin like I had just stepped off a rollercoaster. *Did the school system fail me? Did I just imagine pickles, or did pickles imagine me?!*

My entire life, up until that moment, I thought pickles were an actual vegetable. I imagined them growing on a bush at a pickle farm where pickle farmers would go around picking out the best pickle for the pickle jar.

I accepted that as reality and never questioned it. Why would I? My assumption that pickles were a vegetable separate from cucumbers was a thought that got lodged into my tiny little brain at some point in childhood, then it stuck around simply because nobody ever told it to leave. Until Joe at the hardware store made that entire concept of reality come crashing down.

It's a funny story, and the realization that pickles aren't a unique vegetable didn't negatively impact me. But what other, more nefarious assumptions was I still holding onto? And how did they negatively impact me?

What about you: what societal programming are you letting run in your mind, unencumbered by your questioning?

What pickle seeds are growing in your life?

NOTES FROM THE STUDIO

Throughout this book, I've included snippets of conversations from guests on the *Rewrite the Rules* podcast. These quotes and insights will help illuminate concepts we talk about in the book. If you'd like more information on specific guests featured in these "Notes from the Studio" sections, I'll include contact info at the end of the book.

You *Are* Your Thoughts

When we talk about our thoughts, most of the time we hear one of two things:

- You are not your thoughts

- Your thoughts are what make your life

We're told not to identify with our thoughts, while at the same time being told that the way we think about things controls our lives. Quite the contradiction, huh?

Two of the best self-development books of all time are: *As a Man Thinketh* by James Allen, and *Think and Grow Rich* by Napoleon Hill. Both espouse the necessity of using your thoughts as a tool for growth.

On the other hand, look at a book like *The Power of Now* by Eckhart Tolle which has sold over 2 million copies and proclaims that escaping your thinking mind and living in the present is the key to deep contentment. That book is just as popular as the others, but they make contradictory arguments.

The truth is, both statements are true: we are not our thoughts, *and* our thoughts make our lives. How can that be? Well, in 2005, the National Science Foundation published research on the number of thoughts running in an average person's mind. They found that the average person has between 12,000 and 60,000 thoughts per day. Of those thousands of thoughts, 80 percent were negative, and 95 percent were exactly the same repetitive thoughts as the day before.

Think about some of the depraved and nasty shit you think about on a daily basis. If we acted our thoughts out, we would all be cheaters, murderers, and thieves.

> *"Simply observe your thoughts like water in a river, like clouds passing in an empty sky."*
>
> **—Jaimal Yogis**

And yet, despite the fact that we do not act on them all, we are entirely and 100 percent a result of what comes from our thoughts…especially the ones that hang out for a while and get comfortable. Those thoughts become stories. Stories become who we think we are. When we start to act a certain way for a period of time, the world and our egos reflect it back to us and we start to believe that's the only way to exist. We believe the story we are telling ourselves and our egos are more than happy to oblige. Remember: safety and certainty are their only goals. Mix in some emotion and you now have deeply grooved neurons that have shaped a new reality. All of this now becomes our identity, then our identity gets lodged into our consciousness—often without our consent.

The calculation at the end of that formula becomes who you are until you start a process that will bring the truth closer to the surface.

NOTES FROM THE STUDIO: REALITY IS WHAT WE MAKE IT

"Separating who you are from who you *think* you are is difficult. Every thought is a seed that either gets to grow then die, or it dies immediately."

—**Donald Hoffman**
Professor of Cognitive Sciences,
University of California Irvine

Keep What Works, Exterminate the Rest

The walls of the canyon were smooth to the touch, and cold from the chronic absence of light. A small wren chirped angrily as it darted behind a shrub ahead of me. This place was old and you could feel it. I continued up the north rim trail after leaving my things about half a mile behind me at camp. The sun started heating the air like a furnace as I glanced at its meandering light: 10 a.m. …11? I had no idea as my phone and watch were 12 miles away, tucked under the backseat of the car.

It's times like these—completely solo in the Grand Canyon—that we remember who we are. When time slips away like that in the depth of a moment, you're left with nothing but the reality of you (whatever that is) and the world. Suddenly it's like a computer system processing false ideas about who we are and old files that we kept since mom and dad initially bought it.

I was thinking of how I had interacted with and treated an old flame of mine who I'd spoken to on the drive. Imagining her blue eyes, I had the sense that my ego was keeping me away from her and strangely enough, simultaneously drawing me to her. Perhaps I wanted to be *seen* with her more than I wanted to *be* with her.

The hours are steeped in molasses down there in the canyon. Lounging under the shade of a sprawling cottonwood tree, the processing continued. Past interactions and assumptions, made clear by the circumstance, drew out pride and shame as the truth started to come into focus.

Our job is not to hang onto these assumptions and old patterns of thought indiscriminately. I have a name for people who identify with their ideas about who they think are too much: they're pickle farmers. They're the people who let old assumptions grow like pickle seeds in their minds, until there's no space left for anything new.

Instead, your job is to foster the thoughts you'd like to grow, and ruthlessly kill off the rest.

Let the truth grow.

Some people may look at this process as a manifestation of vile hatred of oneself—that because we have "flawed" thoughts, we are flawed ourselves. But that's not true. When we live our lives according to old thoughts and assumptions, we're simply running on old software. And as you know, software can be updated. A good start to updating that software is to ask yourself this question:

What patterns of thinking do I have that served me in the past, but are inhibiting me now?

This is a hard one, but here's an example of what it might look like:

While not the most outgoing kid on the playground, Olivia always had a couple of close friends that she enjoyed playing with after school and on weekends. From her vantage point, all was normal in her small world. When she was about ten years old, a teacher made a light-hearted comment that she was "one of the shyest girls in the classroom." For all accounts and purposes, she actually *was* slightly more introverted than the other kids her age. Not a bad thing, just a harsh truth for a ten-year-old.

At this point, Olivia didn't even think directly about the comment, the seed merely planted itself in her tiny subconscious and started to grow. It was watered by her brain, which was naturally looking for ways to support that part of who she thought she was now. It kept her safe during childhood and let her enjoy solitude. Over the next decade, it developed into a story and finally blossomed into an identity.

Fast forward 15 years and she moved to New York, where she hoped to pursue her love of fashion and work with a small startup. She had already visited a few of her friends who moved there, and had fallen in love with the new restaurants to try and parks to discover. Autumn in the city that never sleeps was exciting as she found her first apartment and was intent on getting in with an innovative company.

As she started to look for positions and asked a few of her close friends for help in finding work, a few of them arranged meetups with connections in the area. After setting up a time to have coffee, she would usually text at the last minute to cancel. Anxiety would flare up; meeting up with new people was tough for her since she was introverted and shy.

Most positions that she was looking for involved an initial interview with three people...and that scared her subconscious and identity to death. How would a shy, introverted person be able to handle talking to three people, all grilling her with questions?

The first couple months flew by, as they always do, as she continued to work at finding a job but making no real progress. This was something she couldn't quite get around in an industry largely built on relationships.

The holidays came and went, the snow thawed in her

blustery city, and spring started to rouse from its winter hideaway. As everything around her started to change, Olivia's identity and thought patterns remained the same.

One afternoon however, she made a radical realization. Sitting at her small kitchen table in the quiet apartment, sunlight was dripping in through the double-paned window. In front of her was a new journal she had just picked up. She started the process of uncovering.

As the tea started to cool, she began to ask herself more questions:

Why can't I find a job? *I don't know, but it is frustrating me.*

What am I scared of? *Meeting new people and putting myself out there.*

Why am I scared of that? *I won't know what to say. I am going to look and sound stupid. It's hard for me to break out of being shy. What if we run out of things to talk about?*

When in my life have I not been shy? *When I went to*

college and made two friends I still talk to, when I had the courage to talk to the cute guy at the coffee shop last month, when I had a five-minute conversation with the grocery store clerk about Indian food we both enjoyed.

Is constantly telling myself I am shy and therefore cannot do these certain types of things helping me? *Uh…no.*

At the end of her subconscious unraveling, she glanced out the window. She was the same person as she had been when she sat down. She didn't suddenly become a gregarious social butterfly who was going to know what to do in every social situation. She most likely didn't remember her teacher planting the seed all those years ago, either. But she had found it wasn't about changing who she was, it was about altering who she could become. She saw the truth: that she could interact with people appropriately regardless of her shyness. She had given herself space to see the difference between who she assumed she was and who she could actually be.

Looking back, it's easy to see how our patterns of thinking serve us at the time. We then take on those patterns as our identity, repeat the same actions blindly and then rationalize the identical outcomes to ourselves, never questioning their source.

> *"People don't have ideas; ideas have people."*
>
> **—Carl Jung**

But once the thought process no longer serves you, it's time to get rid of it. You can't do this without some gratitude and humility. You needed that thought process at some time; it protected you emotionally. But now that protection is keeping you in a lonely castle, sectioned off from what you really want. In that case, it's time to let your assumptions die off.

The first step is creating some space to recognize what stories and thoughts are still there, stopping new trees from growing. Then you can start to see when that narrative is being played out and replace it with something more constructive.

The "I'm just an introvert" or "I am broke" voice in your head can easily be replaced with "I enjoy making new friends" and "I am in the process of making more money."

If you change the direction those thoughts run through

your mind, it truly can change the course of your life. If you change your life, you can change your community. If you change your community, there's no telling what problems you can solve. So long as you get rid of your most destructive and useless ideas.

Are You a Contrarian for Contrarian's Sake?

Before I became a firefighter, when I was in Ameri-Corps, I'd convinced myself I joined because I wanted to follow my intuition to uplift my community and society at large. At the time, I would've told you I had a deep desire to give back after living a good life up to that point—which was true to a certain extent.

But if I'm being completely honest with you (and myself), that was mostly bullshit. I joined AmeriCorps for mainly one reason: because other people weren't. It made me feel special. Like I was going to volunteer my way to self-actualization. Plus, I wasn't about to go get a basic 9-5 like everyone else. I would be different. I was taking an alternate path because society couldn't tell me what to do!

Except I was wrong. By consciously doing the opposite of what I was "supposed" to do—by being a contrarian for contrarian's sake—I was still using the mainstream as a guide for my behavior. I was still subject to other people's expectations.

Here's the thing: doing whatever the hell we want all the time doesn't make us any more self-actualized or enlightened than just doing what we think we're supposed to. Both extremes are driven by the same core values: values that are *not ours*.

"You can't stop the waves, but you can learn how to surf."

—Jon Kabat-Zinn

So what's the answer—to say goodbye to all trappings of modern life, because the catch-22 is too much to handle, and you're damned either way? *Exactly*. Just kidding.

We don't need to fight the need to fit in, it is a natural human thing. If you only do what you want, you'll end up as one of those hermits who lives in the woods and has names for all the squirrels. You need a community of genuine people, and you can't have that without conforming to a certain extent. We can be rebels from within, but even Mick Jagger has Keith Richards.

And don't believe the people who say they don't follow society's rules *at all*. Those people are doing one, some, or all of the following:

- Faking it.

- Rebelling so hard against the norm that they are still victim to it (I fall into this camp more often than I'd like to admit—as do most teenagers).

- Rebelling against the norm, but only within the confines of their small group identity (cults are an obvious example, as well as ideological zealots).

Whose Standards do You Live By?

When you were in high school, the social hierarchy mattered. A lot. It felt like the jocks would be cool forever, the cheerleaders would be hot forever, and the nerds would be losers forever.

But look at some of those people now. The jocks are selling car insurance (not that there's anything wrong with that), the cheerleaders are selling their multilevel-marketing products (there's definitely something wrong with that), and the nerds have inherited the earth.

If you could've seen where they'd end up, you wouldn't have put so much stock in their social standing in high school. More importantly, you wouldn't have cared about your own social standing either. But my god it all felt so important and permanent back then. They liked you if you made the game-winning jump shot or shotgunned beer like a college student.

Here's the thing: let's say you were a nerd in high school

and you owned it. Rather than assuming nobody liked you because you were a nerd, you instead chose to hang out with the jocks and fit into the social hierarchy. You would have had the best of both worlds. You would have stayed true to the nerd that you were, and you would have had a more fulfilling social life.

This is a microcosm of society itself. The point isn't that we need to step away from society completely. Like the nerd at the cool kids' table, we can still operate within the social structure provided to us—we just have to stay true to ourselves within that structure.

The people we see as visionaries are usually the people who have aligned themselves within the economic and political system of the present, all while staying true to their own habits, lifestyle, and mindsets. Success, in other words, isn't defined by the system created for you—it's defined by the system you create for yourself.

> *"Man does not simply exist but always*
> *decides what his existence will be, what*
> *he will become in the next moment. By*

the same token, every human being has the freedom to change at any instant."

—Victor Frankl

Saws Up

It was early summer in the mountains of Arizona—the beginning of firefighting season. That time of year, fire crews across the country start testing the new recruits. They put new guys through the ringer to see if they're the type of person they can count on. To find out if they'll crack under pressure. To discover what kind of suffering they can sustain. The purpose of this evaluation boils down to answering one question:

Are you legit?

We bounced down a gravel road to the trailhead where we were going to begin our climb. I sat in the back of the truck with my trusty comrades. The classic combo of nerves and excitement coursed through our veins.

We were up almost 5,500 feet and it was full of mixed pine and conifers. The air was crisp, clear, fresh.

The doors of the fire truck swung open, and we all

geared up. I was a rookie, so nobody told me much about the day's mission—my first ever.

Being a rookie, most of the important information lived higher than I was on the hierarchical ladder. By the time it reached me, it was a small piece that the rest of us would do our best to string together in a coherent fashion.

To the best of my knowledge, however, a lightning strike had hit somewhere up the mountain and started a small fire. Our mission was to dig a line around the blaze and ensure it didn't spread.

I wasn't sure I was going to remember to get all the individual gear we had been trained to have on us on the way to a fire. The three other rookies and I did that thing where you do something just *slightly* slower than everyone else—fast enough that you don't stand out for falling behind, but slow enough that you can look around to make sure you're doing it right. I slipped into my dark green pants and fire-resistant long-sleeve shirt. I strapped on my fire boots, slapped my hard hat onto my head, threw some Copenhagen into my cheek, and put my 40-pound pack over my shoulder.

In wildland firefighting, the fire crews don't march randomly. There's a specific sequence of crewmembers, and the most important are the sawyers (the people with chainsaws). They're up in front of everybody. At first glance, this structure seems counterintuitive, since the sawyers carry more weight than the others. You'd think they'd be in the back, where their slower pace wouldn't hinder the rest of the crew.

However, keeping the chainsaws up front keeps the entire team together. The slowest people set the pace, rather than lagging behind, ensuring that the entire crew stays together as a unit. Moreover, when brush needs to be removed, the sawyers have to go first so the rest of the crew can dig a fire line behind them to stop the blaze.

The phrase that still sends excitement and dread through my bones to this day, echoed through the forest before that first mission, and every one after is:

"Saws up!"

And up we went, through the pines in search of a fire and into the recesses of my mind. The real journey never begins underneath our feet, it begins between our ears.

I was nervous as our 20-man crew made its way through scattered trees and up a rocky mountain trail. I felt this overwhelming mix of uncertainty and excitement. I simultaneously wanted to run away and run closer to the adventure sneaking up on me.

As we made our way up, I thought: *This isn't so bad. It's a beautiful day, and the air is nice this time of year. Is that a woodpecker?*

How is this pace? Do I look weak? I got this.

Fast forward 45 minutes, and the walk in the park had transformed into a walk through hell.

Jesus Christ this is taking forever. The air is so thin I can barely breathe. Are we almost there? I could use a break.

But I didn't dare voice these thoughts out loud, for fear that I'd be remembered forever as the guy who couldn't make it on his first fire.

Another 30 minutes went by and my lungs gasped for air.

One foot in front of the other, Alex. You can't let them sense any weakness. Not today.

One of the veterans chimed in from the back of the line:

"Starr, having some issues man? You want to stop, don't you? Looks like you might not have trained hard enough."

Fuck that guy. I started to slow down as the smoke from the fire was still nowhere in sight. How far away could we still be? My mind continued…

Ya you are slowing down, because you aren't cut out for this. See? See? You didn't train hard enough, he's right. You aren't as strong as everybody else.

I slowed down even more, succumbing to what I felt was real.

Just stop already. Make an excuse. Pretend to throw up.

I wanted to give up. I wanted to give in to that voice

like I had done hundreds, maybe thousands of times in my life. Stopping, at least in the moment, is so easy.

I'm not gonna make it. I knew I wasn't cut out for this.

At this point I turned into a zombie: simply moving forward mindlessly, unsure of whether or not I'd collapse at any moment. As the minutes dragged on, I pushed forward mostly from the power of social pressure and not wanting to look weak.

Before I passed out from altitude sickness or exhaustion, we crested the top of the mountain, but nothing made sense to me. I saw no smoke nearby or on the horizon. There was nothing but cold, charred ground snaking between towering pines. There had been a fire here, no doubt about it, but not for a few days—certainly nothing we could fix now.

I collapsed under a tree as I guzzled water. *Why the rush up here?*

The older guy walked up and slapped me on the shoulder. "Welcome to the crew, new guy."

I looked up at him and he smiled.

"What? You didn't think we'd let you into the fire crew without a little hazing, did ya?"

It took me a while to see it, but something shifted in my mind in that moment.

For the years I did the wildland firefighting, I always thought our crew could only move as fast as the sawyers—the ones up front with the chainsaws. Eventually, I realized that wasn't true. Because on that day, my first one out as a rookie, it wasn't the sawyers holding anybody back.

It was *my assumption* that I wasn't good enough that held me back. I could put the blame on the other guys in the crew for making me question myself, thinking I didn't belong. But their hazing never would've worked if I had known beyond a shadow of a doubt that I could make it up the mountain with no problem. Their jeers were all just a performance, but the insecurity they preyed on was very real.

I'm not good enough to do this.

How many times do you encounter something new—whether it's a new job, a new relationship, or a new school—and assume you aren't qualified for it? Only to find yourself a few months down the line struggling to succeed in your new position, constantly fighting in your relationship, or failing all of your classes? Does that happen because you're actually not good enough for them? Maybe. Sometimes the sawyers really do slow you down as you chop down the brush in a new territory.

What's more likely, though, is that you're failing because of your assumption that you're not good enough. And all of your behaviors and actions serve to reinforce that point. In those instances, the universe conspires against you—whether it's the voice in your own mind, or the voices from the people around you.

Our Greatest Strength and Our Greatest Weakness

Worry can eat you up inside, and it's important to know exactly how it does. A 2009 study by Timothy Hartwig explored the costs of mental and physical exertion. The study took a group of college-aged rugby players—big, hardcore musclebound guys—and put each of them on an exercise bike. The researchers conducting the study asked each athlete to produce as much wattage as possible on the bike then let them rest for two weeks.

When they brought each athlete back into the lab two weeks later, they asked the rugby players to complete something called the Stroop test, which is a mental test where color names are written in the wrong color. For example, the word "red" would be written in green, "brown" would be written in red, and so on. Their task was to say what color the text was, rather than read the actual word.

They did that for five minutes, then were put back on the bikes to produce as much wattage as possible. After they'd taken the Stroop test, they produced 25 percent less power on average than their session two weeks before. Their conclusion was that they were able to create less physical power because they'd tapped into the self-regulation parts of their mind to complete the mental test.

Think about that in terms of your own life. When you worry about whether you'll be successful, you use up mental energy that actually depletes your physical output—by at least 25 percent. Therefore, worrying if you will quit or not may in fact make you quit.

But if you blankly go about your business, you're more likely to be able to exert your full physical and emotional capacity.

That means there's a nasty part of your brain-body connection that wants to hold you back. It's like the sawyer at the front of the fire crew, holding you in line, keeping pace so you don't get ahead of yourself. That sawyer inside of you wants nothing more than to stop pushing and to become complacent.

Unless you're open to having a lobotomy, you can't excise this part of yourself easily. You have to make friends with it. You have to talk back to it. It's deep inside of you, and it's so primal that it doesn't know any better than to try to hold you back.

This sawyer was placed inside of you by evolution to keep you safe. You're able to exert less physical effort when you've used mental effort because the sawyers in your mind are trying to keep you from overexerting yourself, just in case you encounter a threat—like a fire—that you need to use your energy to fight off.

But here's the thing, my friend: we live in the twenty-first century. Our brains and bodies haven't caught up to the fact that we sit on our asses and type words on a computer 65 percent of our lives and have so few threats to our wellbeing that we have to go through threat simulations on video games and movies just to feel something.

This adaptability is worthy of our gratitude. After all, it kept our ancestors safe long enough to produce us. But it also hinders us. We can inhabit every harsh corner of this earth, which is a powerful thing. But that adaptability also allows us to rationalize staying stuck in the status quo.

We are so good at adapting that we can become stuck in "good enough" places and situations, convincing ourselves that we're fine. And you know what sucks about it? You are fine. Your core survival isn't threatened by spending a little too much and having just enough money to get by every month, staying at the job you despise a little too long or by stopping your workout one rep short of what you could do.

You can survive that way for a long time.

But can you thrive?

The easy part is making a hard decision to get out of a shitty situation. The difficult thing to do is make that hard decision to get out of a decent situation. This is why most of us are stuck at decent, when we could be at great and making significant progress to where we truly want to go.

The Phantom Leash

My parents had a black lab when I was growing up named Coal, who was known for running away on a whim. He was a real dick about it, too. He didn't physically flip them the finger when he did it, but I swear that in his heart, if he had the manual dexterity to pull it off, he'd have flipped us all off as he ran up the driveway and out of sight.

My dad responded by getting Coal a 50-foot leash that he attached to a stake in the middle of their yard. This allowed him to roam the backyard as he relieved himself or barked at imaginary creatures in the woods. Coal ran back and forth on this leash month after month, season after season. Until one sunny autumn day, my dad hatched up a brilliant idea.

He took Coal outside, tied the running leash to his

collar as usual, but then he did something different: he never attached the other end of the leash to the stake in the ground, just to see what would happen. He left Coal there, unattached, free to run away to his heart's content, and watched from inside. How would Coal react?

He reacted by doing nothing different or out of the ordinary. He went about his business as usual and kept himself within the confines he was used to. Every once in a while he'd see an interesting bird or squirrel, which would prompt him to make a quick, barking sprint, but every time he got to the point where the running leash would usually stop him, he actually stopped himself.

After so much time spent being attached to the leash and having predetermined boundaries set *for him*, the job was done—his training was complete. Coal was no longer constrained by the physical leash. He was limited by the leash in his mind.

I wish I could look at Coal and say that he's just a dumb dog, but you and I are also susceptible to old patterns of movement and behavior that hold us back, just like dogs on a phantom leash.

It's the same dynamic that caused me to walk into that

hardware store asking for pickle seeds—an old assumption or old belief that was working just fine until it wasn't. Then all of the sudden, you're faced with a situation where you have no choice but to realize, "Holy shit. The way I've been thinking about this has been wrong the whole time."

You might not lose out on anything major by walking into a store and asking for a product that doesn't exist. But if we keep ourselves in that arbitrary mental place for too long without questioning it, we forget what our world looked like before the leash was put on.

"It was enjoyable at one point. But after a couple of years you're not that happy but you're also so far into it and there's a line that you cross when all of a sudden it becomes the norm for you, this is how it is. You might've forgotten what life could be like as the months turn into years. And once it becomes your new life, it's hard to change.

"I remember one day just mindlessly staring at the computer doing accountant books that I didn't like. And it just hit me. I realized I don't want to do this anymore, and I don't have to. I started taking the steps to change my situation that night and never looked back."

—**Kyle Holsinger** *who had a Masters Degree in Business and a plush accounting job for years before quitting to pursue his dream of being a firefighter*

CHAPTER 2

You Were Created to Be Safe

"Realize that sleeping on a futon when you're 30 is not the worst thing. You know what's worse, sleeping in a king bed next to a wife you're not really in love with but for some reason you married, and you got a couple kids, and you got a job you hate. You'll be laying there fantasizing about sleeping on a futon. There's no risk when you go after a dream. There's a tremendous amount of risk to playing it safe."

—Bill Burr

They were falling like matchsticks.

It was Central Alaska at the peak of summer and one of the largest fires in the country roared through the thick and remote conifer forest. We had flown up from Phoenix on July fifth on a large jumbo jet, along with three other crews from around the country to help the local Alaskans fight the fire.

Alaska is so massive and settlements are so sparse that most people allow the fires to do what they were designed to do: burn, uninhibited. But this time was different. They only called in reinforcements like this when fires got out of control. And this fire was definitely out of control.

From Anchorage, our 20-person crew took a school bus to an off-the-grid village where lumbering grizzlies and moose were frequently reported in the area. That's where we set up base camp for the next three weeks.

Every morning, we caught a chopper from this remote camp and were swept off to a specific section of the fire to contain it and ensure the main section did not roar back to burn new areas. Riding the helicopter never became routine to me. When you shoot across the sky in a fire helicopter, there's a certain destructive beauty in the contrast between the calm, enclosed space you inhabit, and the head of an orange blaze, eating across the horizon, shooting smoke a mile high into the atmosphere.

Chaos on the outside and peace within.

Aside from the fire, the landscape was as beautiful as it was monotonous—with evergreen trees carpeting miles of rolling mountains. I only knew we were close to our landing zone when our pilot, a confident guy with a Hawaiian Islands sticker on the back of his helmet, would begin maneuvering broad, controlled loops as he spiraled us down to earth.

As we made our approach, the surrounding air swirled with dirt and ash from the downdraft of the chopper blades, cushioning the soft landing of an experienced pilot.

We hustled out of the chopper, grabbing our chainsaws, extra fuel, tools, and rucksacks—enough supplies to last the night, just in case of an emergency or if the helicopter malfunctioned and couldn't pick us up on time that evening. We were about 10 miles from the nearest small settlement.

As a leader-in-training, I was in charge of an eight-person squad that looked to me for the best way to complete the mission at hand: secure our section of the fire and leave it cold—zero chance of spreading. I was in a leadership position, sure, but I had no clue what I was doing.

I was disproportionately concerned with how my squad perceived me. As such, I alternated manically between being overly demanding with my commands, and being too soft and laid-back to compensate. The thing was, most of the guys on my squad had been my peers for the past three fire seasons. We'd shared enough beer-fueled escapades that any time I barked a command, I'm sure they couldn't help but think, "Does Starr think we don't remember him pissing in that mailbox last summer? Why should we listen to a mailbox-pisser?"

Looking back, I have no idea if anyone was actually thinking anything close to that. But still—during the first few days of the assignment, I had this internal voice assuring me that a *real leader* would come along and save me.

That voice finally hit a crescendo when a single pine tree changed everything. Like the burnt wick of a candle crumbling into the wax, the fire had weakened this pine tree to a char, causing it to fall. It came down with a crack, directly at Luke. All we could do was scream in the brief second before it came down and grazed the hard hat he was wearing; a foot in a different direction would have seriously injured or killed him.

The area we were working in was full of these small pines that were burnt, just like the one that fell. I hit the radio to alert my superiors of my plan to make sure something like that didn't happen again.

"This is Starr. We just had a small pine come down and slightly hit Luke. No injuries, but we can't risk anything, especially as winds pick up. We're gonna take 'em all down and go from there."

A static-filled response from the Captain: "Copy that, do what you need to do."

We proceeded to cut down every single tree that looked even remotely suspicious. They were already dead, but it still felt like a massacre. The aggressive screech of chainsaws rang through the forest as they spewed wood chips onto the black, barren ground.

We cut and cut until our collective breath grew heavy and deep. Finally, there were only two trees left: large, beautiful, healthy pines that stood defiantly like twin giants on the now-empty hillside.

One of our sawyers took off his hard hat and wiped his brow with his forearm. "Whatya say, Starr? We cuttin' these two or not?"

I looked at the towering pines. They appeared untouched by the fire. It seemed senseless to cut them down—the fire had already wreaked enough havoc, and so had we in its wake.

"No," I said. "These two stay."

Exhausted from the rampage, we sat down for lunch. We found a comfortable spot in the shade of those two pine trees and scarfed down sandwiches from our packs. There's a certain depth of hunger that hits you when you're living in the Alaskan summer—where the sun never sets, and the work starts at 4:30 a.m.

We relaxed in the delight of a job well done. I felt particularly proud of myself as a leader for making the job safer for the crew while saving those two pine trees. I imagined a future where they'd act as the spores to repopulate a new forest in the barren landscape around us.

Suddenly, there was a loud cracking. As we looked up, we realized what was happening: the seemingly healthy pines were falling in our direction—fast. We made quick moves to the left and right, then hopped back to the spot where we'd started just as the two trees fell on either side of us, shaking the ground with a thunderous rumble.

If somebody had slipped or if the trees had fallen just a couple feet in either direction, somebody would've had to start the chainsaws again just to cut the logs and recover our pancaked remains.

Luckily, nobody was hurt. But I've thought about that moment many times since that day. I think about how close we were to having everything go terribly wrong. I wonder why, in the midst of every other tree falling down, I thought those two trees would be fine. I think about my arrogance as a leader, which could have killed us on that long, summer day.

I realize my mistake now. I assumed that because those trees had green needles, strong bark, and large trunks that they were healthy. But those trees didn't fall because of their branches and leaves. And they certainly didn't fall because of their bark or the way they swayed in the breeze. They almost killed us because of their roots. See, in that part of the world, pine tree roots can only grow about four feet down to a permanent layer of cold dirt called permafrost. I had taken those trees at face value, when in fact they were unstable underneath.

Where else does that happen in life?

When we think of our family ancestry, the tree is the most common metaphor (that's why we refer to it as a family tree). But sometimes, like those pine trees in Alaska, you're not given a chance to root yourself deeply into the earth. The reasons may be as ancient as the millennia-old permafrost in those mountains, or they may be as new and as urgent as a forest fire.

Either way, there are certain modes of living that are

imposed on us—whether environmentally, socially, or from our parents—that don't set us up to succeed. More often than not, those modes come from good intentions. Our parents teach us to get a good, stable job because they don't want us to take the risk of starting a business or "wasting" time with creative pursuits. We're taught to go to college because it's more accepted than using that would-be tuition money to become an artist, a traveler, or a jack-of-all trades.

They're all noble and, at times, helpful impositions. I am not suggesting we entirely give these up either, but simply question their motives. Who do these thoughts and ideals come from, exactly?

They have percolated through multiple layers of history and structure but at the end of the day, they're largely predicated on one desire: to keep you safe.

And ironically enough, those impositions are the very things that keep you from rooting yourself deeply and confidently into the earth. They make you unsure of yourself. They stop you from blasting through the permafrost; in the end, the mindsets and habits that were meant to keep you safe will have you crashing down to the ground like a pine tree in the forest.

The Perils of Comfort

"Humans don't mind hardship, in fact they thrive on it; what they mind is not feeling necessary. Modern society has perfected the art of making people not feel necessary."

—Sebastian Junger

In the twenty-first century, human beings in developed countries can have *every* need met by walking about 20 feet. Every. Single. Need. Never before in the history of humanity has this been the case.

A possible morning:

7 a.m.: Wake up under the blankets. Walk 10 feet and press a button with a finger that turns the temperature up a few degrees in the house. Ahh, perfect. Time to shower.

7:15 a.m.: Walk another 10 feet and make the arduous move of bending over, extending the right arm, and then doing something a little extra: turning a knob instead of pressing a button. Once the knob is turned, water (the most valuable resource on earth) comes spewing out of the faucet. Now you have to wait for it to warm up.

7:16 a.m.: Walk three feet over to the sink where yet another knob is turned to let a small amount of the most valuable resource on earth land on a small brush that you use to rub against your teeth.

7:18 a.m.: Teeth properly rubbed, time to stand under a faucet near the ceiling that will—for an extent of time that is entirely up to you—pour warm water on your body as you rub the rest of your body. Relaxing. No need to light a fire and get a certain amount of water warm, just stand and soak while you think about the problems in your life.

8 a.m.: Walk out to a metal machine and press yet another button to allow entry. The key was getting to be too much work. Sit down on a comfortable chair and yet again, press a large button which initiates a sequence that rapidly combusts gasoline and oxygen within a confined space to move four wheels at a precise moment. Whatever, you need more money.

8:02 a.m.: The sun hasn't fully crested the horizon, so the car is a little chilly from the night. No problem. Reach down and press a few buttons that start to heat up a piece of glass in the front and the interior of the personal moving metal machine. Much better.

10 a.m.: Shit! Forgot to bring a lunch and you have so much work to catch up on. Take a look at the cellular device and come to decision paralysis as you figure out not only what app to lightly tap on your device but also what area of the world you want your food to be based on for the midday meal. Finally decide on Korean food. After the decision, you open a leather booklet and pull out a small piece of plastic. You type the numbers into your cellular device and—doing things completely unknown to you or the majority of people on the planet—it transmits those numbers as data across literal and digital space which enables you to order your meal.

That is just the morning. And that's just the need for shelter, food, and water. We haven't even started on the list of wants. That list is never-ending.

We've never had more opportunities for growth and improvement than we do now. And yet, we still find it hard to take risks and truly transform ourselves, despite the overwhelming options available to us for jobs, education, romance, etc.

Why?

Well, let's hop in the old time machine and head back there to find out. Our collective history holds a few secrets that help connect our core hunter-gatherer genetics to our modern lifestyle, and how those discrepancies keep you from becoming who you need to be.

First stop: 1850. The Industrial Revolution is in full swing. Smoke billows into the atmosphere, people are moving from rural towns to urban centers, and for the first time in all of human history, people are being treated like literal cogs in a machine. Let's step onto a factory floor real quick. Look at all those people assembling widgets, over and over again. Do you think the factory manager knows each of them by name? Not likely. Do you think he cares about their hopes and dreams? Nah. These people are not inherently valuable in this factory model—but the totality of their labor output most certainly is. Let's get out of here before we catch tuberculosis or depression.

What do you think—a hundred years in the future? Yeah, let's do that. Let's stop in 1950 and see what post-World War II America is like.

My God, what a difference a century makes! Look at

all those cars, and homes, and dear lord, are those what I think they are—suburbs?! Compared to 1850, this is paradise. Turns out, prosperity reigned supreme in most of the post-war world. After the global conflict of World War II, most of the world's superpowers needed friends to help them clean up the mess. Trade agreements were signed, peace became the norm, and the proliferation of the television transformed the way we shared information and entertainment.

All of these factors coalesced into the creation of the American middle class: a growing group of people who had stable income, the means to purchase consumer goods, and the money and credit to make it happen. Whereas the poor factory cogs in the industrial revolution had to fight tooth and nail just to survive, the burgeoning suburbanites achieved two things no other generation in human history had ever benefited from so much in such great numbers: safety and comfort.

That meant middle class families could make purchases not solely based on need. They could buy things just because they wanted to. The tectonic shift resulting from so many people having disposable income for the first time in history is often overlooked, but it completely changed the world in ways we still don't understand today.

However, one side effect we're sure is from this new middle class is the "keeping up with the Joneses" phenomenon. I mean, just look over there, down the street of this quiet little suburb. That's your grandpa, if you can believe that. He's washing his 1945 Chrysler Imperial. It's a really nice car, but check out that sideways look he's giving his neighbor, who's hosing down his beautiful, brand new, mint green Bel Air convertible.

You already know what happens next. Even though your grandpa has a perfectly good car of his own, he's gonna buy a new one, just to keep up with his neighbor. And soon enough, after he buys that new car, that one won't be good enough anymore either, and he'll need another, and another, and another, never realizing that more acquisition of material goods won't result in any more fulfillment.

The Hedonic Treadmill

Philip Brickman and Donald Campbell researched and created a phrase for this human phenomenon of constantly striving: the hedonic treadmill. As soon as you acquire the item, the promotion, or the new lifestyle you wanted and derive the requisite pleasure from it, you'll soon become accustomed to it and desire the next thing. It becomes impossible to feel fully satisfied.

This phenomenon itself isn't shocking. What's shocking is that we have so many resources that this could actually become a problem. Imagine telling those people in the fertile crescent thousands of years ago and in those factories of the 1800s that in the future, their descendants would live such comfortable lives, that one of their major problems would be having too many things.

That Industrial Revolution factory worker would be so bitter they'd probably throw their porridge at you. On an evolutionary level, our progress happened too fast—our minds haven't caught up to our wealth. On a more immediate, familial level, your grandparents and parents were products of an economic revolution that helped large populations of people acquire wealth like never before. Naturally, they wanted to pass that wealth down to you—but they passed on even more. See, your grandpa over there has a lot to lose. He was a kid during World War I, he and his parents lived through the Great Depression, and he was an adult during World War II. The safety of the '50s is a welcome reprieve from the chaos that colored his life to this point. He doesn't want to lose that, and he sure as hell doesn't want his children to face the same struggles. So he passed that hedonistic treadmill down to your parents, who lived their lives trying not to lose the safety and comfort they'd been given, rather than seeking out more truth and adventure.

Then guess who they passed that on to? You.

And with the stakes so high, who could blame them? Whether they know it or not, their values are old hand-me-downs that date back to post-war America, the Industrial Revolution, and the first Neanderthals to ever get eaten by a wild predator. They all lived their lives by a single credo:

Don't take unnecessary risks. If you do, you will die.

That value and those patterns of behavior were handed down to you from your parents and your evolutionary ancestors as a means to keep you alive. And those values will save you if you encounter an alligator in your apartment complex.

But whose values are you enacting when you prioritize

the safety and comfort of the life you live now over the potential for something better?

Nothing Else Needed

It was a beautiful pine tree. Early summer in the Colorado mountains and I had nothing to do on a dreamy Saturday as I neared the end of my service year in AmeriCorps. The mountain air was still cold so I would put on my one pair of Levi's, a cotton T-shirt, and a Carhartt jacket. I really didn't have many material things except a few clothes, my favorite book, and worn-in boots.

There I was under that tree on that particular day, laying down with my eyes to the vivid blue sky. Pine needles crunched under the weight of my back as I rested on the slight slope. I told myself to remember that moment forever. That I was so full with simply living, I didn't need anything else. Instead of my usual habit of constantly projecting into the future, striving and waiting for the next chapter in life where I thought it would finally start, an elusive peace settled in for a few moments.

What would the world become if all of us got off the

treadmill and let those moments stick around for a while? Instead of getting to our grandpa's age and living the same safe life, chasing the same dopamine rushes, and deriving the same false sense of comfort from a life that has been carefully constructed to keep us from remembering the fact that we are all going to turn to dust soon.

How *You* Keep Up with the New Joneses

Any time before the nineteenth century, most people only met a few hundred people in their entire life—if that. Now, in the twenty-first century, you can be exposed to the opinions and creations of thousands of people every single day.

This isn't all bad, of course. This influx of opinions and perspectives opened the door to massive cultural shifts in relationships, work, food and how we live our daily lives. These shifts have transferred creative power to you, the individual, who can now create and distribute without waiting for someone else's permission to do so.

However, you are constantly being influenced by these multitudes of people and opinions on a level that has never been seen before in human history. We're all on a search for an antidote to the madness this influx of stimulation has caused.

It's no coincidence that yoga, mindfulness practices, and a psychedelic resurgence has become more popular in the west at the same time as the technological and information revolution. These are the counterparts to the digital age. This is our humanity we are looking for.

We fear that if we don't keep up with the Joneses we'll be ostracized from our community. This is our worst fear as humans: to be cut off from the rest of the tribe. We're hyper-social creatures. If we're ostracized, we die.

Advertisers and marketing firms have been exploiting that fear since we were born. And it's how they get us to keep buying things: because we think without their product, we won't fit in.

Happy, content individuals don't make very good consumers. They have no iPhone-sized hole in their hearts. Therefore, advertisers don't have a lot of incentive to make you feel happy and content. They don't want you focused on the moment. They want you achievement-focused, so they can convince you that you can't reach your goals without their products.

A society built on consumerism that is full of content, happy individuals soon collapses. This is why psyche-delics have remained obscure and illegal for so long. They have the potential to disrupt the social order by helping people see the truth… that they probably have way more than they need to be content. It may be closer to what we all want but it does not fit with the current paradigm of the system already in place.

Your parents and grandparents used to look at their neighbors to keep up with the Joneses and fit in. Now you look at strangers on Facebook and Instagram to keep up with them. That's your hedonistic treadmill: the habitual cycle of consumption that gives you the false illusion of comfort and security. How do you break that cycle?

Fail.

Cut Down the Biggest Motherf*cker in the Forest

There's a right way to cut down a tree, and a wrong way. Here's the right way: you start with a triangular cut on one side (that's called a pie cut because it looks like a slice of pie). Then you make a single, horizontal cut from the back that sends the tree crashing to the ground in your desired direction.

Here's the wrong way to cut down a tree:

It was late February in an expansive section of Pike National Forest in Colorado. I stood there in two feet of snow with an 80-foot pine tree looming above me. I was still a rookie, and it was my job to fell this tree safely.

Two words that never go together: *rookie* and *safely*.

I knew as much about making a pie cut in a tree as I did about baking a pie at home—zilch, nada, zero. Sure, our crew captain had told us about it, but I didn't want to look like a stupid rookie, so I didn't ask questions. I just cut away. And it almost killed me.

Firing up the chainsaw, I went to town on one side of the trunk, sending wood chips flying onto the snow like pinewood confetti. Pie cut looked good, everything was solid and ready for the final cut to have it fall to the north.

"Tree coming down!" I screamed, as was required for safety when cutting near others.

The teeth of the chainsaw gripped the back of the pine as I started into the final backcut. I glanced upwards through the billowing branches and grey backdrop to see what the tree was doing. At this point, it should have started to slowly lean in the direction I had been planning on but I saw no movement.

Come on...do something. I could feel my captain's eyes on me. It was 35 degrees outside but I felt like I was in a sauna.

God damn it why isn't the tree moving?

A slight breeze picked up, gently pushing the 5,000-pound pine in the opposite direction, which pinched the saw under its incredible weight. This situation is one you hope never happens: 80-feet of pine over you, halfway cut, possibly falling at any moment, and the one tool you had to help is now stuck in the tree itself.

The snow continued to drift as my captain walked over, grinned through his grizzly beard, and said, "Well, what are you going to do?"

At this point, he explained that the only option was to borrow his chainsaw, cut on the other side of the tree to get it to fall that direction, and not kill myself in the process. Sweet.

Taking a deep breath of the icy air, I began the cut that would either make me a hero or flattened to the side of the mountain. The plan seemed to be working as the saw dug further and further into the rich wood. I glanced upwards and saw movement, yes! The tree finally cracked free of its trunk and fell to the ground with a loud *boom* and a puff of snow. My captain didn't say anything after the tree fell, but I knew based on the look he gave me when he handed back my chainsaw that he was thinking, *You almost killed yourself, rookie.*

I was shaken by the almost-disaster I'd narrowly avoided. Luckily, it was time for lunch, but my hands shook so bad I could barely eat my sandwich without dropping it into the snow. The incident replayed over and over in my mind. I thought of the dopey confidence I'd felt cutting down the tree, having no idea that a few more seconds would have spelled my doom. I started to doubt my abilities.

I'm out of my element here. I'm gonna get myself or some-one else killed.

I wanted nothing more than to pack up my chainsaw for the rest of the day and move to another job on the crew. Anything but cutting trees. But my captain had other plans.

"Starr. Grab your saw and come with me."

I wiped my hands clean and grabbed my chainsaw, practically having to jog to keep up with him.

"I know that first miscut is always scary. You wanna run away. You're probably wondering how you can get through the rest of your career without cutting down a tree again. That right?"

"Oh, no. Yeah, it was a bit dicey for a second there, but I'm good to go."

"Right. Scared shitless, just like I thought. No shame in that. But let me tell you something I wish my captain had told me when I was a rookie: you don't run away after a miscut like that. If you do, every tree down to a sapling will overwhelm you. You know what you do instead? You find the biggest motherfucker in the forest and cut it to the ground."

He'd led us to a charred giant, even taller than the one I'd miscut before lunch.

"Go to work," he said.

I fired up my saw. My hands shook. No longer from fear, but from a rumble of determination emanating from my chainsaw into every bone in my body. I had to get back on the horse and go to work before my nerves could grow that horse into a dragon.

Like a surgeon, I narrowed my focus squarely on my incision point. I sliced through the trunk to make a clean pie cut, then I moved to the other side and gave the giant its fatal blow, sending it careening to the ground exactly where I wanted it.

My captain nodded in approval. He slapped me on the shoulder and walked away like nothing had happened. And by God nothing did happen. Because my captain had taught me an important lesson that day: when you make a bad cut, you don't respond by packing up your chainsaw and going home. There is only one way to bounce back after a failure and build true confidence in yourself. You go find the biggest motherfucker in the forest and chop it down at the knees.

The Failure to Fail

If I'd packed up my chainsaw that day, I would've fed the anxiety and nerves in my mind. My actions would have said, "You're right to be scared. You stepped beyond your competence level and look where it got you. Never again."

How many times have we done that in our lives?

- You talk to a cute girl at the bar and she rejects you, and you respond by not asking out any more girls that night.

- You take a buzzer-beating shot and miss, then you decide you'll let someone else take the next one.

- You go on one job interview and make a fool of yourself, so you take the safe route by only applying to jobs you *know* you'll get.

What if, instead of running away after a failure—which

feeds it, and makes it loom larger in your mind than it really was—you leaned into it even more? You responded to the rejection by the cute girl by asking out another girl. You take another game-deciding shot. You apply to another job you're underqualified for.

You'd reinforce something important to yourself: that failure doesn't control you. You control your failure. Even if you fail a second time, it would still be a victory. Because you're proving to yourself that you didn't let it cripple you.

It's Real

For years, fear of failure kept me from trying hard at anything. If I tried hard, then I might put in a great effort only to get mediocre or bad results. My fragile ego couldn't take that. Imagine studying your ass off for a test, only to get a B– on it. Now imagine you barely study and get a C on the same test. Which result is better?

Looking at it objectively, you'd say the B–. But that's not what you internalize as a kid. That B– is a way bigger hit to your ego than the C, even though it's a higher grade. Why? Because the C has a built-in excuse: "If

I'd actually tried, I could have gotten a better grade." But you don't try, which allows you to keep your true potential not only ambiguous in your mind, but also untapped. If you try your hardest and get a B–, that's concrete—you see that as your complete potential, and that may feel like a failure.

So what do you do? You don't try hard because you are afraid of failing. The mindset follows you like a ghost, tainting everything you touch.

This cycle of self-protection leads you to consistently fall below your potential:

- You don't try your hardest in your creative pursuits, which guarantees they aren't as good as they could be.

- You don't put too much time or effort into your work, so you always underachieve professionally.

- You hold back in your love in relationships, never fully giving yourself to anyone so you can avoid heartbreak.

Follow this formula for a few years and you'll soon discover that if you don't give everything, you are left with almost nothing. Everything will be half-assed and microwave ready. Distractions and blue light will soak up your day like a dry towel until there is nothing left. Soon, everything you do is designed to help you save face and keep you from risking embarrassment. So you sit in the safety of your comfort zone, never trying or risking anything, and as a result you gain nothing at all.

When I think of this phenomenon—the tendency to never try your hardest for fear of failing despite your best efforts—I think of vultures in the sky. I think of floating on a remote lake on the border, sometime in the middle of summer. I imagine the sun on my face, beating on me from a sky that's as eternally blue and as tepid as the water I float in. I spot the V-shaped black wings of vultures cruising overhead—these creatures that dine on death, occupying a space between this world and the next. They're purgatory creatures. When we stay in that safety, we become a purgatory creature like them, caught between who we are and who we could be.

Your parents raised you to protect yourself, the same way they tried to protect you. What life would you live if you no longer held onto the illusion that you are protected at all, and instead let yourself float on the waters of life, confident that you would never make it out of here alive?

YOU WILL RESIST WHAT YOU NEED MOST

The door on the small and beaten down old car would shut and close out the world, letting a strong silence fill the space.

I had just finished AmeriCorps and moved back home, aggressively saving money so I could move at the drop of a hat for a firefighting job through the US Forest Service, wherever they might need me. In the meantime, I was working with a local storage unit company. I spent my days sweeping hallways, cleaning up shit from the homeless people who used some of the units as temporary homes, and plotting my future.

During lunch breaks, I'd sit in the car and eat my turkey sandwich. Then I'd pull out a large and tattered black journal full of the names and phone numbers of captains at every wildland fire station I was interested in working for. These seemingly random collections of letters and numbers might hold the key to my future as I had heard that it helped to speak with them on the phone or in person so that your application does not get lost in the bureaucratic shuffle.

All I had to do was actually dial the number and talk.

There's only one problem: it's damn scary.

For days, I couldn't bring myself to make any calls. I'd eat my sandwich, read a book, call a friend, then stare out the window. I would do anything besides pick up the phone and call them.

Calling friends was much safer than calling fire captains. I imagined these giant, bearded men in a cabin deep in the woods, chopping trees down with axes before lumbering inside to a breakfast of potatoes, coffee, and Copenhagen (actually quite a good combo I would later discover). There was me, sitting in my dad's old car, fresh from cleaning the shit somebody left in the storage units, and living at my parents' house. I had no money, and zero certainty that my life was going to turn out OK.

Why would some strange lumberjack man want to talk to me?

What would I even say if they answered?

What if I worked my way down the entire list of names only to realize I screwed up my odds by calling them rather than just letting my application speak for itself?

Days turned into a week. Then two. Then, in week three, I couldn't take it any longer and I called the first number on the list. My heart pounded as the phone rang. Relief washed over me when it went through to voicemail.

A lady answered the next phone number, but she told me to call back another time.

I mustered the courage to call a third number.

"Hello?" The man's voice embodied everything I'd been afraid of: it was gruff, hasty, and to the point. I swallowed as I wondered if this lumberjack man was about to chew me up and spit me out.

"Hi, is this Captain Stevens?"

"It is."

"Hi. I'm Alex Starr, and I'm interested in applying to be a wildland firefighter at your station. Is it alright if I ask you some questions?"

Something magical happened: he responded—like a normal person. He said he'd be happy to answer any questions I had.

By the end of my conversation with the captain, I didn't have a job, and I never did work in his station. But I had made the call.

The next day I sat down in the same spot to make the same type of calls and expected to be entirely free of that feeling of anxiety. Instead I found the exact same voice waiting for me, sounding happy to have me back. As I reached down for the journal again, I had a moment where I realized it was never going to leave, I just had to continue to act in spite of it.

Your Resistance

The same way you were raised by your family and society to be safe, your mind also evolved to keep you safe. That's why I had what Steven Pressfield calls "resistance" to making that phone call. It is a mystical force that wants to keep us where we are to keep us safe. Our limbic systems (aka our lizard brain) can't distinguish what's good for us and bad for us.

When you want to take a risk, even if it doesn't pose any real danger to your personal wellbeing, your limbic system still steps in and says, "Woah there, cowboy. Let's hold up a minute. You already have food, water, and shelter. What do you think you're doing? Talking to that cute girl isn't worth it, and you definitely shouldn't pick up that phone and make that scary call. Don't do it, it's not worth it!"

That voice holds you back, and the little bastard will follow you around your entire life, the same way it's followed mankind around for millennia. It wants nothing else than for us to stop what we are doing, stop pushing past where we are to become who we want to be. Progress, in the face of this resistance, means death. Death to what is clearly working (you being alive).

The thing is, unless your physical wellbeing is actually

in danger, your mind and this force will greatly over-estimate the risk involved.

This is the same force that keeps you eating crap food you know isn't good for you, the same energy that ties you to your job or the relationship that sucks. You know you want to get out…but something is holding you tight. It is this resistance, the vortex of your own ideas about who the hell you think you are. What you think others think you are.

It thinks it's doing something noble by trying to keep you safe, but it's an outdated system.

Some of these possibilities that are brain constructs as being "terrible" (no matter how unlikely or how they actually help us learn to grow and expand) tend to loom over us like storm clouds. They might ruin our day or week. But what is a bad day, really? Let's break it down and make it explicit using a tool our caveman ancestors didn't have the luxury of employing: math.

If you live for 75 years, that means 5 bad years—and I mean bad, where you have no job, no friends, you're living in your parents' basement eating nothing but

Doritos and cereal, and you're worse off at the end of it than when you started—is only 6.67 percent of your life.

When you're talking about your entire life, 6.67 percent is no joke, but it's not 67 percent. And that's 5 years. Do you know how unlikely that is that you'll have 5 black hole years in a row like that, and that you'd learn *nothing* and be no better on the other side? Losing 6.67 percent of your life to a bad five years is hardly a death sentence.

A bad year—again, 365 straight days of pure misery—is only 1.33 percent of your life.

A bad month: 0.11 percent of your life.

A bad week: 0.02 percent of your life.

And a bad day, where everything you can possibly imagine goes wrong and you don't know how you'll wake up in the morning and do anything ever again: 0.003 percent of your life.

Seeing the numbers behind this, part of me was excited to use this math as an excuse to sit my lazy ass on the couch and watch TV, scarf pizza, and drink beer for weeks at a time. I'd proclaim myself a math god, victor over my biological ancestors and vanquisher of the limbic system.

However, it's just a mental exercise to show you that:

1. Truly bad days are incredibly rare, because everything bad that happens is an opportunity for growth. And...

2. Even if you did have a bad day, month, year, etc., it's a shockingly small percentage of your life.

The only reason you don't want to take risks is because you've been protected your whole life. You won't be able to out-logic a neurological system that's evolved over hundreds of thousands of years, but you can do the next best thing—you can see it for what it is: an echo from a past that no longer applies to you.

Sure, listen to that part of your brain if you're flying down the freeway at 100 mph on a motorcycle, or standing on the edge of a cliff at the Grand Canyon. In those cases, your limbic system may actually save your life. But when it tells you to stay safe and comfortable when you want to write that script you have been talking about for years or start getting back in shape, just recognize what it's really doing to you.

It's eating your life away, training you to avoid black hole days, all while living in bland comfort and mediocrity. It's stealing away your chance to be the kind of person who takes risks and finds growth where others find failure. It steals that from you—one tiny fraction of a percent at a time.

> **NOTES FROM THE STUDIO:**
> **STEP OUT OF YOUR SAFETY BOX**
>
> "It was just a lot of fighting myself for years on this decision. Action sometimes doesn't happen until things become really uncomfortable and you get to a place where it's do or die, you have to do something. And that was the point I had reached. I had to do something or live miserably the rest of my life. So I finally started looking into it as a serious option, and that was terrifying because it was actually becoming real...and that is always the scariest part."
>
> —**Laith** *on his eventual decision to start the process of taking testosterone and transitioning from a woman to a man*

Tend to the Roots and Build a Forest

"But there are moments when curiosity gets the better of fear. I guess for me such a moment had arrived."

—Michael Pollan

Waking up on a summer evening, a thin veil of sweat was clinging to my skin. The soft, repetitive hum of the fan kept the room from being perfectly still. *I can't put this off any longer,* I thought to myself as I staggered to my feet and onto the cold tile. It was finally time.

The motorcycle and I cruised toward our favorite bar on the Mexican border. The Arizona sun was sinking into the horizon, and I was full speed ahead trying to run from the critic in my mind. We pulled up to the rustic spot; I cut the engine and walked in. Three beers later and I finally had the courage to do it:

I hit publish on my first podcast episode.

I wish I could say I went down there to bury a body or hide some money, and that's why I was so nervous. But no. I just wanted to muster the guts to finally get my podcast into the world. Who knows why I felt the need to go down to the border to do it—maybe I was hiding from something?

After I hit the button and it was live, I sat on the patio of this seedy bar, and nothing happened except a light breeze of the Arizona night wind. Nobody told me congratulations. The bartender didn't give me a free drink. I didn't get a phone call.

Nobody cared in that moment except me.

Nobody congratulates you when you first step out of your comfort zone. In fact, if you do it right, a lot of people may be mad at you. When you take that first plunge into the unknown, it makes people uncomfortable—even the people you love. Whether it makes them realize they're not taking a plunge in their own life or they're worried you'll get "too good" for them, risks can put you at odds with others.

So we have to do it for the right reasons.

It took me over a year to muster the courage to post that podcast episode. Was it because I didn't have it recorded? Absolutely not. Did I not understand how to upload the file? No.

It was because I was afraid. I wanted to take a risk and be safe all at once.

So what'd I do for the year leading up to that moment in that dive bar at the border? I toiled over the logo. I agonized over the name. I tinkered with the website. On and on I went, hiding in the details when the only thing that mattered was getting the podcast into the world. I focused on the branches of my podcast, rather than tending to the roots: the fear lurking beneath my desire to grow.

Of course my real problem wasn't finding the perfect logo. That much is laughably obvious at this point. I was scared to put it out into the world. I was scared of taking that leap, then having people listen to it and think it sucked. Newsflash: it did suck. It was recorded on an iPhone with an old friend of mine. She was great but I didn't know how to keep a conversation going or what questions to ask, and you could barely hear us over the choppy audio quality.

But when you're sitting on the porch of a dive bar in the dry night air near the border, it doesn't matter how good that something is. What matters is that you made it and took the risk to show it to other people.

At first, nobody will care except you. And it may be a lonely feeling. But if you keep with it, and tend to the roots instead of the branches, you won't just have a single beautiful tree.

You'll have an entire forest of creations that people will be drawn to.

Why Fish Can't See Water

"Give me the child until he is seven, and I will show you the man."

—Aristotle

At the end of the day, nobody...and I mean nobody... knows what the hell is going on here. Two-year-olds are fresh from the other side. Ninety-year-olds are about to go back. Everything in between is ours to discover.

When we're children, we're all little Sherlock Holmses. We listen to the people around us, absorbing our native language. We watch how our fellow family members behave, seeking models for our own behavior. So although we have a lot of genetic similarities with our fellow humans, we were all imprinted with different cultural, familial, and behavioral norms from the time we were born. Some of which have nothing to do with your individual personality.

If you were born in the Mongol Empire in the thirteenth century, you would've been a herder in the Eurasian Steppe, using falcons to hunt and traversing across the land to withstand warring tribes.

If you were born to an Aboriginal Australian tribe in the eighteenth century, you might have believed in a deity called the Rainbow Serpent, and you would have played the didgeridoo.

If you were born a woman at the turn of the twenty-first century in Saudi Arabia, you would have been expected to wear a hijab to cover your face and you wouldn't have been allowed to drive.

If you were born in North Korea under one of the Kims, you would have lived a life of Orwellian dictatorship and perhaps not even known the difference.

Hell, even in your own country, in your own time, there is a wild buffet of possibilities. You could have been born on the same day in the same country as someone else, but depending on your family, your living situation, and your socioeconomic status, you might have grown up on a farm with working class parents who expected you to be a farmer like them, an immigrant in the inner city, or you might have grown up in Miami to affluent parents who paid your college tuition.

With all of those factors converging into one human being (you), it's easy to get lost in what you think you're *supposed* to do.

This isn't a curse, it's simply a law of nature to contend with and manage instead of it managing you.

The easy way out is to say, "Fuck all of it." To resent the fact that you're influenced by your culture is as futile as resenting the fact that you were born: maybe you have reason to resent the circumstances of your birth, but it doesn't answer the question of what you're going to do about it. Instead, I'm challenging you to take the harder path. The path where you recognize how your values and perceptions have been molded by your upbringing, and work to change them from within.

You weren't just raised to be safe—you evolved to be safe. It takes a lot of work to overcome that. And, if I'm being honest, you don't want to overcome it completely. It's one thing to power past your fear of launching a new business or reaching out to somebody you haven't spoken to in years. It's another matter entirely to stupidly risk your life or the people around you, doing something like, oh I don't know, letting two pine trees crash and almost kill your entire wildland firefighting crew.

At a certain point, you have to find the line between the parts of you that keep you safe out of necessity, and the parts of you that you were passed down out of fear from your parents, your culture, or your ancestors.

All of those fear-driven heirlooms in your DNA can and should be cut down, mercilessly. They're like the charred pines of an Arizona forest, waiting to be felled after fire has ravaged their roots, leaving them primed to come toppling down, allowing space for a better life.

CHAPTER 3

The Whisper of Your Instincts

The nightclub pulsed with Enrique Iglesias's "Bailando" playing on repeat. It was approaching 3 a.m. in Antigua, a weekend destination outside of Guatemala City, and I was dancing with a friendly local with long dark hair. Antigua was popular with tourists and locals alike because it was usually safe from the gang activity that plagued its big-city neighbor.

Key word: *usually*.

It was closing time, so the entire club spilled into the

cobblestone streets, enveloped by the dark beauty of the sprawling mountains surrounding us.

My dance partner smiled at me. "What are you doing with the rest of your evening?"

"I don't have any plans," I said.

Her face lit up. "Well, some of my friends are having a party. You should come."

At this point in my life—in my early twenties—whenever a girl wanted me to go home with them, I always thought I was the butt of some joke. *Am I on a hidden camera prank show?*

She knows it's just me under here, right?

"You know what?" I said. "I'm in."

"Awesome! Our friend Carlos will drive."

Decisions like this are what can make or break an evening. They can make or break a life if you let them. One simple decision to go home with the wrong person, stay at that job a little too long, never quite get the courage to ask that special somebody out, say no one too many times. We were about to find out to which path this decision led.

I squeezed into the back of an old, beat-up SUV with my dance partner. It was the two of us in the back seat, Carlos driving, and another guy in the passenger seat. As we drove out of the city, the three of them were laughing and having a good time—speaking Spanish, which I barely understood. My instincts started chirping in the back of my mind. I told my instincts to shut up so I could listen to my dick instead, which had led me into this stranger's car in a foreign country where we were careening down back country roads, out of the city toward an undisclosed location.

Your mind plays some interesting tricks in moments like that. If you haven't listened to your inner voice for a long time, you'll easily drown it out with other bullshit. Your perceptions become skewed and you make bad decisions, like a game show contestant.

My grandma used to watch *The Price Is Right* every afternoon when I was growing up. I loved seeing the cool prizes people could win and how excited they got to meet good old Bob Barker. He would always announce the products they could win with a particular zeal:

"Right here is a beautiful set of golf clubs, perfect for that balmy spring day when the greens are cut short for your putting pleasure!"

"Andddd over here is the brand-new picnic table. This table boasts four seats and the option of an umbrella for entertaining with friends and family this summerrrrr!"

It took me a long time to realize that all the lights, sounds, and beautiful models were part of a calculated formula to heighten the contestants' emotions. And once they were in that heightened emotional state, they'd become flustered, lose track of their common-sense instincts, and make bad decisions.

When I got in that SUV, I was in my own heightened emotional state, transfixed by the pretty girl, the bright lights, and the possibility of winning my own prize. I imagined Bob Barker unveiling two future versions of me like game show prizes ready for me to win:

"Behind curtain #1, we have Alex back home in America. This spontaneous version of Alex got into a strange

SUV in Guatemala and not only lived to tell the tale, he actually had sex with the man's female friend! He comes fully equipped with validation from his friends, and the self-perception that he is adventurous. No risk is too small for this Alex—he traverses the globe soaking up every ounce of fun he can find, no matter the consequences."

"Aaand behind curtain #2, we have the lovely corpse of the former Alex Starr! Nevermind the smell, this young man lived a terrific life for a quarter century. That is, until he made one dumb decision that ended it all. Who knows how many adventures this version of Alex gave up to enjoy one night of almost-fun in the mountains of Guatemala?"

"Which one will it be?"

Away from the bright lights and loud music of the club, I finally listened to my gut. I had to get out of that SUV.

We bumped along a dirt road toward the mountains outside of town, winding through the darkness. As we did, my dance partner started running her hand up my thigh. The fire alarm in my mind rang louder than ever. I contemplated my options: open the door and roll out, strangle the driver from behind, pretend to puke and ask them to stop—none of them were ideal. Then the passenger up front bailed me out.

I knew enough Spanish to know that he said something equivalent to, "Hey Carlos, let's stop and grab some beer."

Thank fucking god, I thought.

We pulled into a little convenience store in the middle of nowhere and the passenger guy got out, leaving just me, Carlos, and my dance partner. She gave me a twinkly eyed look.

"I need to get some fresh air," I said.

Before she could answer, I opened the door. I started spewing keywords at her, hoping she'd get the picture without me explaining—*home, tired, walking.*

She was disappointed. "What? No, please stay. We just got beer!"

The more she insisted I stay, the more certain I was that I'd wake up without my kidneys in the morning if I did. I ran off into the night, eventually finding my way to my little casita in Antigua, hours later—alone and kidneys intact.

I'm all for living a life of adventure, and I firmly believe that seeing the world as a big opportunity for adventure is a big part of overcoming fears that have held you back. But that doesn't mean you should ignore your instincts.

As you step off the path that your parents, ancestors, and society laid out for you, and you get on the path that you set out for yourself, you may come to a similar realization that I stumbled on that night in Guatemala:

I'd forgotten how to hear my instincts.

Don't put yourself in a dangerous situation where you're forced to listen to a voice in your head that you've ignored for years.

The Answers Are Inside

His name was Ben. My bitchy manager at the storage unit constantly told me to kick him out. He couldn't be there so much, she said. While he wasn't technically living there, he would spend hours in the unit a day, and I would often catch him napping on an assortment of old clothes and dirty boxes.

The guy was obviously on drugs, trying to get clean from drugs, or constantly thinking about drugs. He had that twitch about him. The semblance of a man who knew what he had become, the thread of reality and his former self was still there, trying to hold on above him. I think that made his situation worse. He could still see and feel the other side of who he was. Other addicts had gone so far out in left field they couldn't see home base anymore. But not Ben, and that's what made it particularly difficult to have conversations with him. I could still see the other guy he could have been.

We each have these two people inside of us. Circumstances, random chance, and the decisions that we make all come together to form the foundation of who we become and how we live our lives.

I firmly believe that a big reason escapist activities like the substance addiction that plagued Ben are on the rise is because people have lost touch with their instincts. In other words, we've lost touch *with ourselves.*

And when we lose touch with our own instincts, when we don't take the time to hear ourselves, we make dumb decisions—even dumber than getting in an SUV at 2 a.m. with a group of strangers in a foreign country.

But what are you afraid you'd find if you actually listened to yourself?

We all have parts of us that we're unwilling or unable to face. Those parts are like the gnarled roots of a tree: if you let those roots grow wild, they might take over the entire forest, suffocating every inch of life.

Who knows what's growing under there?

- Maybe you're resentful about your brother being more successful than you.

- Maybe you're following your dad's vision for your life instead of your own, and you don't even realize it.

- Maybe you regret not trying harder in high school.

- Maybe you can't love others because you know deep down you really don't love yourself.

Whatever those gnarled roots may be, they have this uncanny ability to seek out the potential for growth in other areas of your life and choke them from below the surface, out of sight and out of mind, leaving you wondering why the hell you're not living the life you want.

The thing is, you will never find your instincts in a book, a new partner, or in a pile of money. Nothing you do *out here* can affect those roots under the surface.

You have to set everything else aside, grab a shovel, and dig deep below the surface of yourself, fighting through the tangled mess of your life to make sense of it all.

In other words, you have to do exactly what you've been avoiding your entire life.

I have searched for perfection under every rock and lover under the sun. I looked for contentment at the bottom of a bottle, in the next dusty town, or a new song. I pried and prayed and meandered and sang to the moon to bring happiness to my doorstep.

But we will never find it out there, for it is inside: the last place we all want to look but secretly understand.

NOTES FROM THE STUDIO:
MANUELA AND SAM

Manuela and Sam decided they wanted to expand their understanding of the world. The two young women bought and refurbished a sleeper van (which they named Raul) and drove it south of the border from Texas, all the way to Brazil.

"It wasn't all sunshine and rainbows," Sam said. "There were multiple times when both of us didn't think we could follow through on it. My family convinced me it was too dangerous and too reckless. Then I talked to Manuela and we said, 'screw it. We're taking this trip for ourselves, and if we don't hop in Raul and drive him down to Brazil, we'll regret it forever.' So that's what we did. And it was life-changing."

Manuela piped in. "If you really believe in doing something, and your instincts compel you towards it, then you can't listen to other people. That voice in your head has to be louder, and you have to listen to it. Life is too short not to."

When I meet people like Manuela and Sam, I always marvel that they're able to rewrite the rules of their lives without any hint of hesitation. Even now, I always hesitate whenever I transform some part of myself.

But once I talked with them on the podcast, I realized that no matter how strong your instincts are, and how loud that inner voice is, you'll still hear the chirping from the outside. Don't listen to them. Every time you take a leap of faith, it will be met with resistance from the outside. Don't sabotage your leap by adding internal resistance too.

Do You Even Know What You Want?

"People arrive at a factory and perform a totally meaningless task from eight to five without question because the structure demands that it be that way. There's no villain, no 'mean guy' who wants them to live meaningless lives, it's just that the structure, the system demands it and no one is willing to take on the formidable task of changing the structure just because it is meaningless."

—Robert M. Pirsig, *Zen and the Art of Motorcycle Maintenance*

Don't beat yourself up about not being in touch with your instincts. Modern life is literally designed to pull us in a million different directions every day. The best behavioral scientists in the world don't sit in ivory towers writing papers for academic journals. They're on the payrolls at Instagram, Reddit, YouTube, and every other social media platform, trying to steal your time and attention away from you.

Perfect example: Kevin Systrom, the co-founder of Instagram, majored in Symbolic Systems at Stanford, a program focused on reimagining the connection between mind and machine.

Social media platforms have also taken some tricks of the trade from casinos, the fairy godmothers of time-wasting addiction venues. Consider the way you refresh a social feed on your phone. You grab from the top of the screen, yank it down like a slot machine lever, and wait to see the jackpot. Sometimes you get three red cherries, a picture of an attractive person or location and sometimes you get nothing. That unpredictability is actually part of the addiction: it's a psychological phenomenon called intermittent reinforcements. The feed is designed to be endless because they don't want you to stop scrolling. And you're more likely to keep scrolling if you only get rewarded on an inconsistent basis. It keeps you sitting in the chair, gambling your way through the social media casino.

We become entranced scrolling through our feeds, like we're members of a cult, listening dumbly, slack-jawed, as our Supreme Leader spouts his incoherent nonsense, punctuated by brief moments of brilliance. Social media is our new, instinct-sucking religion.

You will encounter a lot of people—whether it's in a massive corporation or in a small group like a church or your family—who will try to steal you from yourself. They will work to take your attention and time away. In the case of companies like Facebook and Google, they will spend billions of dollars to figure out how to do it.

You have to be diligent. You have to get in touch with your instincts and discover what you want, not what others want for you. Otherwise, you will lose yourself— literally, figuratively, or some disastrous mix of both.

Life Is Loud—Quiet It

A hundred and fifty years ago, there were no social media platforms to get addicted to.

In 3000 BC, there was no Christianity concept to follow. In the middle ages, a time-sucking television would have been witchcraft. But that doesn't mean people in other eras were completely pure, innocent, and unencumbered by their time.

At some point after World War II, the economy picked up again in America. Just like we talked about before, it was easy for people to make good money with a stable job, and they could afford to buy a nice house in the suburbs with a picket fence. It didn't look like it at the time, but these cultural shifts were setting up a story in the American psyche:

Life comes in little predictable boxes. The box of my safe job. The box of the 45 years I'll work from age 22 until 67. The box of my fenced yard behind my cookie cutter house in my cookie cutter suburb. The box that my new refrigerator came in, paid for exclusively with credit. When a national mindset like that dominates a culture without anyone even noticing, it can insidiously pervade every facet of life. Eventually, we aren't sure if we really want that safe job and predictable future, or if we're simply living out a recent string of social paradigms and a collective consciousness we happened to be born into.

> Everything you do can fit into one of these three categories:
>
> 1. What you want
> 2. What society wants for you
> 3. Some mix of the two

It's hard to see the system of the moment because it's so loud and pervasive. The assumptions of our time are embedded in every piece of media, every conversation, and every advertisement, to the point that it drowns out your own thoughts.

The solution: quiet down that noise, reboot your brain, and start digging through the roots of your mind.

The Brain Reboot

Refamiliarizing yourself with your instincts isn't as simple as cutting out social media. It requires something deeper and more involved. Having said that, I want to point something out: social media platforms don't make a lot of space for "behind the scenes" views of people's lives. You're more likely to get attention for flaunting your ass or showing off your latest vacation. Nobody posts a picture from their latest breakup, or that time they were constipated, or a selfie of them having an existential breakdown at 4 a.m. Instead, you post pictures of the tree of your life in the most beautiful light, leaving the roots underneath hidden.

And here's the kicker: I don't think you only hide those roots from the rest of the world. You hide them from yourself. When you hide those roots from yourself, you can't get to the bottom of who you are, what you want, or where you're going.

In order to do that, you need to reboot your brain.

Get Rid of the Noise

SIT ALONE WITH NO PHONE

Out of the 4.5 hours an average American has in free time every day, we spend about 3 hours and 15 minutes of that on our closest friend, the smartphone.[1,2] We don't realize how addicted we are to the phone until

---

1   McClear, S. (2019, November 03). A new study shows that Americans actually have plenty of free time to exercise - they'd rather just spend it on their phones. Retrieved from https://www.businessinsider.com/new-study-americans-free-time-exercise-phones-2019-11

2   Matei, A. (2019, August 21). Shock! Horror! Do you know how much time you spend on your phone? Retrieved from https://www.theguardian.com/lifeandstyle/2019/aug/21/cellphone-screen-time-average-habits.

you get rid of that dopamine machine. Setting it aside works like an apricot face scrub for the brain: It resets priorities and reminds us that whatever is happening on the phone and social media is not real life. In fact, in a lot of ways, the definition of "real life" is everything that's *not* happening on the phone.

When was the last time you left your phone untouched for a full 24 hours? It sounds so simplistic, but the results are anything but. Having a No Phone Day is an excellent way to dam what may feel like a constantly flowing river of anxiety and doubt in your life. You need to quiet that roaring river so you can hear the whisper of your intuition.

JOURNAL

The memories we can contain of seemingly nothing and everything. The fog and the sadness and the joy and the love of the beginning and the end. How do we reconcile these parts of ourselves? These memories that are buried deep within our subconscious and crave the light. The feeling that we know we don't even know. That we can never know. The irreconcilable recognition that everything that has already happened will never

be happening again. How do we deal with such existential realities?

These human ordeals can be loud. Life can be loud.
Your job is loud. The to-do list is loud. The replay of
what you could have done better in the past is loud. The
stress about the future and how it will turn out is loud.

Netflix, family emergencies, the wants of your significant other and/or friends, the phone. All of these things
conspire to create this massive glob of noise constantly
nagging your inner dialogue.

More importantly, they're all external. Journaling is a
fantastic way to get beneath the surface of yourself and
see what's really going on. It's like creating a map of the
gnarled roots in your life.

How do you journal?

It's simple: sit down, either on your computer or with a
notebook—whichever is easier to start—and just write
whatever you're thinking, without censoring yourself.
Nobody is ever going to read this (most likely including
you), so there's no need to be grammatically sound or
make sense. In fact, the more rough it is, the more likely

you're getting to the root of who you are. You can also use a few prompts to get started:

- What are you proud of?

- How do you feel right now?

- Who do you admire and why?

- Write a letter to your high school self.

Again: is journaling simple? Absolutely. But it's also powerful and deceptively difficult. The key is to start by doing it badly and just keep going forward with it. An easy way to start is to pick a day every week when you keep your phone on airplane mode, and choose that as your journaling day to start. Then you can ramp it up from there. You'll be shocked how much better you get at hearing your intuition and knowing more concretely what you want if you do that.

> "Following your bliss," is a great line for selling books, Instagram posts, and throw pillows but in the end, life will still suck sometimes. We all want a recipe for heaven without burning the pan.

> Journaling is a great outlet for that eventual downturn which is all part of the rhythm of existence.

STOP COMPARING YOURSELF TO OTHERS

Comparing ourselves to others is one of the most insidious habits that we normalize. The reason comparing yourself to others is so detrimental to your health is two-fold:

1. It either puts the other person on a pedestal, or...

2. It puts *you* on a pedestal.

Either way, you're feeding your insecurities. By comparing yourself to others—whether looking at them with envy for having the body, person, car, or life you don't, or by looking at them with disdain for not having what you have—you miscalculate. You see yourself only in terms of how you stack up against others.

Comparing yourself to others is an old social gauge that goes back to our chimp ancestors. You set your limbic system into overdrive, and you dig into that deeply wired tendency to calculate your place in the social hierarchy and do everything you can to raise it.

Perfectly natural? Sure. But you have to ask yourself if you want to live your life as a simple product of evolution—which was largely chosen for you—or as a product of your conscious choices.

BEHIND THE MUSIC

Every major advertiser and media outlet in the world knows about our desire to compare ourselves to others. And guess what: they use it to their advantage, and your disadvantage, every day.

I love the behind the scenes features on shows and movies. Like most people, I want to see the underbelly of it all. I want to see the truth about the people we've placed up on a pedestal. It's the same reason why biographies and documentaries about famous people always top the movie and book charts. We all crave the truth.

What are these powerful people like in their daily lives?

What do their days look like?

How have they fucked up?

Really what we're asking is: *How are they like me? How can I relate?*

There's nothing wrong with being curious about other

people's lives. That's perfectly natural. Trying to fight against that would be as futile as fighting against your urges to eat and have sex.

What I'm talking about is comparing your complete "behind the scenes" view of your own life with a polished, highlight reel version of other people's lives. That just leads to false perceptions, resentment, and the desire to watch others fail.

The Difficulty of Nothingness

We all have a deep resistance to the quiet of our own minds. Who wants to dig up the gnarled roots of your life to see what's hiding under there? It's scary. The thing is, there's a part of us that *wants* to be distracted from that discomfort. That's why it's so easy for us to sink into Netflix and social media for hours: because deep down we yearn for that escape.

We hide from the discomfort of hearing our intuition because we don't want to hear the uncomfortable truth:

You're not living the life you want.

We hide behind trite motivational lines like "Follow your bliss," or "All you need is passion," or my favorite

"If you love what you do, you'll never work a day in your life."

It all sounds good, but it's actually bullshit. Even if you're living at your deepest purpose and trusting your instincts every step of the way, you'll still think about the future. You'll doubt what you're doing in the moment. Your relationships will go to shit sometimes. And ice cream will still taste good.

Distractions—the loudness of life—will never go away. But at your deepest core level, there's a part of you that never changes and never goes away either. It's the part that makes you who you are, despite the fact that your physical makeup—down to the cellular level—has completely changed over the decades of your life.

That deepest, unchanging part of you is the whisper you try to hear in the midst of the loudness of life.

It's funny how easy it is to lose touch with ourselves. It is one of the greatest ironies we experience as humans involved with our egos instead of our intuition. It can completely take over our lives until we are being dictated to, and pulled around by fleeting desires that were most likely given to us, not decided by us.

Suddenly we aren't where we wanted to be and the place we are at feels like it will last for eternity and nothing can save us. Life is loud, intuition is a whisper. It's already there, waiting for you to listen for a second and uncover what you already know.

Can you automatically hear that whisper if you turn off your phone and journal? No, not necessarily. But you have to start somewhere and give yourself a second. Once you do hear that whisper, it will be painful. You may realize that you've been chasing your tail your entire adult life (highly likely). But after that pain, you get to move forward from solid ground and healthy roots.

Stillness in the Rush

Dave was a recovering drug addict and alcoholic with the tattoos and insightful personality to match. We would drive around to various restaurants and businesses that would donate their leftover food to the food pantry where Dave worked, and where I was volunteering during the first project of AmeriCorps.

Bumping across the roads in a rickety van from the nonprofit, Dave and I would talk about a wide range of things as we crisscrossed Denver on those grey, winter days.

After about a week of this, we had built up enough of a relationship where I felt I could ask him a question that had been on my mind.

"When was the moment that you realized you had to get sober?" I inquired.

Will he get pissed? I wondered. Maybe reminding him of the moment would cause him to cry or even worse, suddenly revert back to his old lifestyle while we're still in the van. *How far are we from the nearest liquor store? Is that how this works?* I didn't know.

He paused for a brief moment before replying, "I almost killed somebody. I got so hammered one night that I left the bar and remember driving down the road. Next thing I know, I am waking up to blood dripping down my face and my car smashed into a tree. I really could have killed somebody, maybe a child or a husband or wife. Only through the grace of God was everyone OK."

A few seconds of silence as the cold air whistled through the cracked window.

"I couldn't have lived with myself if I had killed some-body. I went and got help immediately after that and haven't looked back. It was the wake-up call I needed but didn't want to see."

Why do we not check our bank accounts when they are low?

Why do we not confront the other person when we have an issue to bring up?

Why not admit when we screw something up and regret it?

Because that would make it real. We would rather live in a fantasy land a lot of times than own up to the fact that we didn't handle our money very well last month.

Who wants to hear the truth? I don't know about you, but I'd much rather avoid my problems than face the harsh reality of why those problems exist in the first place.

Belly me up to a no-name bar on a forgotten highway, and I'll drown those problems for a night, only to watch

them re-emerge the next day, stronger and more prom-
inent than ever.

We could become more present, successful, and happy
in the world if we acted from our intuition, and yet it's
so difficult. Instead, it's easier to act from our egos. That
part of us that wants to be perceived as cool. That part
of us that doesn't want to show everyone the gnarled
roots underneath our lives. That part of us that would
rather be seen with an attractive partner than open our
hearts to them.

Every time you want to escape, ask yourself what it
is you're hiding from. Sit with the question. You'll be
shocked at what you hear in return.

Why am I procrastinating on this project? Because I'm
afraid of success.

Why do I put myself in dangerous situations? Because I
don't think I deserve happiness.

Why do I keep choosing bad relationships? Because true
intimacy scares me.

That's the only formula to getting in touch with your intuition:

- Recognize when you're trying to escape something.

- Ask yourself what you're escaping.

- Listen to the response you give.

- Sit with that response.

There's no magic ending to the formula that automatically integrates that intuition. You have to grab the shovel, dig under the tree, and look at the gnarled roots head-on before you can do anything else.

A fantastic and well-proven way to do this is through the increasingly popular, free, and magical movement known as meditation. Donald Hoffman, who I had the pleasure of speaking with on my podcast and has been referenced throughout the book, explained it best:

> *"Meditation begins at the limits of objective reality, at the farthest point yet reached by rational knowledge and perception. Meditation thus does not mean rejection of objective*

reality; on the contrary, it consists of a pen-
etration to deeper dimensions of reality. It is
not escape into an imaginary dream world;
rather it seeks after the comprehensive truth of
objective reality, by simultaneous, stereoscopic
contemplation of its surfaces and depths."

You can start by closing your eyes and counting a few of your breaths. Download "Calm" or "Headspace" and give those apps a go or read a book on it. It doesn't matter what you choose but choosing *something* that helps get back in touch with *you* is all that matters. It can be meditation, a walk in nature, surfing, journaling, microdosing shrooms and laying in a hammock, listening to music, creating art, or making banana bread. Just pick one that gets you "there."

Once you see those roots of who you are more clearly, the path forward will be more obvious.

CHAPTER 4

The Most Important Thing

"An old friend will help you move. A good friend will help you move a dead body."

—Jim Hayes

The world's longest road is the Pan-American Highway, which stretches 19,000 miles from Alaska to Argentina. However, somewhere in the wild jungles of Colombia, there's a 70-mile gap—an expanse of tropical forest that's too dense and too full of leftover Colombian guerrilla fighters to build through. It's known as the Darien Gap, and it has baffled explorers since the sixteenth century.

It was late February and I was 5 months into the fire-fighting offseason and 4 months into a South American journey, traversing around doing my best to learn Spanish and volunteer/work my way from country to country with a backpack.

There are plenty of sites that have postings from around the world with locals offering free room and board in exchange for help or volunteer work such as building a school, tending a farm, nannying, or construction. I had come across a fascinating post looking for help building a hostel in the tiny coastal town of La Miel, Panama which lies directly on the border of Colombia.

As I and three others left on a small prop plane from Panama City, the buildings quickly disappeared as we made our way across vast and dense green jungles, eventually landing on a strip of dirt near a few small houses.

Once we got as far as we could go with our tiny plane, we were quickly herded onto a very small and narrow boat. The guy in the back who was manning the small motor must have been around 80 years old with leathery skin and a rugged personality. He whisked us around the cape, effectively sidestepping the treacherous jungles on land as we bobbed across massive 20-foot swells in the ocean. A petite, elderly Colombian woman clutched her rosary and prayed for our safe passage next to me the entire time.

Finally, we arrived at our home for the foreseeable future: a single-story concrete structure on the beach. Inside were eight other travelers from around the world and a few hammocks for us to sleep in. Our payment for building this hostel was nothing more than free room and board while we did so.

As I settled in, something didn't seem right. I zeroed in on the most experienced-looking person in the building. I asked him how things were going so far.

"Could be better. The owner's stuck in the states for a family emergency, I think he said."

"Holy shit."

"Yeah. It's like *Gilligan's Island* here. We're basically fending for ourselves during the day, then there's a local caretaker who comes by to make coconut rice and fried plantains in the evening. Could be worse."

There was no electricity, no running water, no cell service, no internet. We had to hike two hours through the thick and uncontrolled Colombian jungle to get to the closest town. There we found the faintest Wi-Fi signal imaginable and a few provisions to hold us off until a local would come by to make us coconut rice for dinner. We spent our days building a hostel—even though we knew nothing about construction—and seeing who was faster at climbing palm trees. Our nights were filled with building massive bonfires on the beach and peeling back the layers of reality with the help of ayahuasca and a local shaman.

It was surreal. As you can imagine, a scenario like that brings you close to the people around you extremely quickly.

Some people left after only five days. Some people stayed there the full three weeks like me. But no matter what, if I saw any of them tomorrow, I'd still have a bond with them that has never disappeared, even years later.

Why? Because despite our relatively short time knowing each other, we had gone through experiences together.

Those profound and intense experiences created strong relationships.

Humans were designed to foster bonds through shared experience, especially ones that can be considered new or a struggle. It would take 50 dinners to build the same connection that could be made playing on a soccer team with somebody for 5 games.

Alonso, a friend of mine discussing his former gang life on the podcast said this:

"When I think about what made it so powerful was that these guys were down for me. I was down for them. We had been through shit together and made it out the other side. It was a family man."

Whatever we decide to do in this life—and there are thousands of options—it will be easier, you will enjoy it more, and you'll live longer and healthier with strong relationships as a main component. At every step of the way, having people we can rely on, open up to, and share our lives with will enable us to move forward in the direction we choose.

The Grant Study

In the middle of the Great Depression, Harvard scientists embarked on a scientific endeavor known as the Grant Study, which would eventually transform our understanding of health and wellbeing. They tracked 268 Harvard men and their children (about 1,500 people in total) over the course of *80 years* to discover how early-life experiences affect health and aging over time.

It turned into one of the world's longest studies of adult life, and eventually included Boston inner-city residents as well. The findings were fascinating, to say the least.

It wasn't money, fame, social class, IQ, or even genes that predicted a long and happy life. It was close relationships. This finding proved true across all groups: the Harvard students, their children, and the inner-city Boston residents. In other words, you might be better off in the long term focusing on calling your friends more often than focusing on cutting down your cholesterol.

Point is, we all have basic needs—such as food, shelter,

and water. And too often, we don't include meaningful relationships in that list of basic human needs.

Make as Many Connections as Possible and Filter Accordingly

First things first: what I'm talking about here is connecting with other people and making friends, *not* networking. The difference? Connecting with people comes from a place of genuine mutual interest. Networking comes attached to an agenda (we'll talk about agendas in a minute).

The word networking can feel sleazy, it makes a lot of people uncomfortable, and it's a disconnected concept. You're not meeting people to "network." You're meeting them to connect.

Except for maybe 1 percent of people, meeting new people will always be at least slightly uncomfortable and anxiety-provoking. Here are common thoughts that still go through my head:

How do I sound?

How do I look?

The conversation is hitting a dead space. What should I say? Do I have a good question on cue?

I don't think I'm smiling enough. Now I might be smiling too much.

I am bored and want to talk to other people, how do I end this conversation?

There are so many things to think about. At a certain point, it's easier to skip social interactions altogether and just stay home on a Friday night. Recognize that a certain measure of discomfort and anxiety comes with the territory when you're connecting. Everyone deals with it on some level—you're not alone.

> Part of this anxiety stems from the sheer complexity of another new human. People and our relationships to them are so complex that our neocortex is thought to have developed significantly just to keep track of them.

If you're uncomfortable meeting new people, don't compare yourself to an extremely extroverted and charismatic person. You know the person I'm talking about, the one who can work an entire room and talk to literally anybody and have them laughing in seconds.

You don't have to be that person. You have your own social strengths so let's figure out how to put them on display.

The best way to play to your strengths and make genuine connections with people is simple:

Go into every new interaction with no agenda.

The Agendaless Agenda

If you have an agenda when you meet someone new, you'll probably have a bad interaction. If you don't have an agenda, you'll have a better and more natural interaction.

That's it.

The sleaziness you feel with networking is a result of trying to *get* something from the other person, rather than just being yourself. Whether you're on a date, buying a car, or asking for help at the grocery store, our selfish desires tend to dominate most interactions throughout the day.

Instead, if you go into every interaction without an agenda, you'll be far more natural and likely to connect.

No agenda is your only agenda.

One of the main culprits of bad social interactions is not just having an agenda, but having a hidden, uncommunicated agenda. Think of the girl who acts like she wants a fling when she really wants a relationship. Or think of the guy who signals that he wants to settle down when in reality he just wants to get down.

When you meet somebody at an event, backyard BBQ, a party, or any place where the parameters of the dynamic are not clearly defined, it freaks you out, whether you admit it or not.

The reason is primal in nature.

In a scenario where we don't have a concrete hierarchy in mind, our neocortex—the part responsible for such things—is forced to figure it out on its own. This is a stressful process because it leaves a lot of room for perceived manipulation and distrust. In other words, the unspoken agenda at most events is that everyone wants to see where everyone else fits in the hierarchy.

It's a lot to handle, even if you go into a social situation with no agenda. It's enough to scramble your circuits, leaving you blathering and confused like a teenager.

LET'S TALK BOOZE

I'd be remiss if I didn't at least mention booze in a chapter about building relationships. We use alcohol as a social lubricant, and for good reason. It eases your inhibitions and makes it easier to talk to new people.

We are nervous about going to a happy hour with new friends or meeting our significant other's family for the first time and turn to it for alleviation of the subtle anxiety.

But everything has a payoff and with alcohol, it's a slippery slope.

Instead of dealing with the anxiety about talking to an attractive girl or a potential friend, you douse yourself with alcohol. At the end of the day, alcohol gives me, you, and society as a whole, one simple thing: **an excuse**. An excuse for not doing what we know we should do but ARE SCARED TO DO. This is the foundational reason why alcohol is easy to grasp onto. Why any substance can be easy to grasp onto.

Why endure the hardship, the trials and tribulation, potential rejection, agony of embarrassment, discomfort of expansion and eventual deep contentment of fostering a genuine connection with another human when we can take the bridge to instant pleasure town?

It's not about being a prohibition-era Puritan who thinks we should eliminate alcohol, it's way too much fun for that. I'm just saying that alcohol can be a healthy social lubricant, but you need to be aware if you're turning it into a crutch that you need to foster genuine connections.

Making Friends

How many genuine friends do you have?

Not acquaintances, who you only talk to twice a year. Not a colleague or business contact, with whom your intimacy only goes as deep as their coffee preferences.

I mean *friends*—no more, no less.

Your answer is incredibly important, because your overall quality of life is a direct reflection of your relationships.

Surround yourself with acquaintances, and your whole life will feel as shallow as an acquaintanceship.

Surround yourself with work friends, and your whole life will feel like constant work.

But surround yourself with people who can be there

on a good day and are always there on a bad one and your entire life will grow as deep and as meaningful as a true friendship.

Here are a few principles I follow to help in the early stages of making new friends.

1. EVERYONE IS A FRIEND UNTIL PROVEN OTHERWISE

Innocent until proven guilty isn't just for the court of law. It's also for the court of friendship. One of the biggest social superpowers you can learn is to treat everyone as a potential (or current) friend, until they do something that proves otherwise. Until then, focus on what would make them a good friend, not what would cast them into your relationship graveyard.

I'm not saying you should be naive to the point of letting strangers sleep on your couch, loaning money to some guy you just met, or inviting a girl you went on one date with to meet your parents. Not at all. I'm saying to err on the side of assuming someone is a friend first and focusing on the good in them instead of waiting for the bad to appear.

Which leads to the next principle…

2. MAKE AS MANY FRIENDS AS POSSIBLE, THEN FILTER ACCORDINGLY

Once you have all those people in your life, you can see how they behave. Do they swing from the chandeliers, sing too loudly, slosh ale like a drunken sailor, and dance like a madman? Or do they speak politely, bow with reverence, and move with grace?

Based on your own values, you can choose which type of person stays in your realm and which one goes. It also depends on the stage of life, how you are changing and evolving, and the dynamics of each relationship.

Point is, you won't know who people really are just by standing in a spire, telescope in hand, watching them at a distance. You have to mingle with them. Workout together, eat together, and maybe commit a misdemeanor or two and you'll eventually get to know them.

Then, once you do, you can choose whether or not to keep them in your life. I've found that to be a *way* better process to build a social support system rather than just assuming everyone is an asshole and waiting for them to prove otherwise.

I've had new friends who lasted 10 minutes before I

started getting strange vibes from them and decided to gently escort them out of my life. Are they still my friend? No. Were they my friend for those 10 minutes? Sure. No harm no foul.

3. SAY YES...TO *EVERYTHING*

NOTES FROM THE STUDIO:
JUMPING FROM HELICOPTERS

"But the thing is, it's just getting in the habit of saying yes. Saying yes to new things and to trying new things. Cause eventually, when we get into the habit of not just being afraid to say yes to eating new things or meeting new people, we will eventually say yes to the bigger things that require more risk. It's good to start by practicing with the smaller things. The noes you get now will make the yeses down the road that much more valuable."

— **Yes Theory:** *a movement started by three guys whose mission is to show others how to seek discomfort to find the truth in life. They have over 600 million YouTube views and one of their videos involved bungee jumping out of a helicopter with Will Smith over the Grand Canyon for his 50th birthday.*

Jim Carrey is one of the most prolific comedy actors of all time. In 2008 he put out a silly yet deceptively profound movie called *Yes Man*, where his character says yes to everything that comes his way in order to get out of a rut he is in with his entire life. I decided that would be me for 30 days when I first moved to Austin, Texas with no network, no job, and dwindling funds. If I wanted to get where I was headed, it could only be done by doing what I normally wouldn't and repeating it until it was more a mindset than a decision.

So I decided that no matter what the event was or how much I didn't want to go, if someone invited me to something, I would say yes.

Let me tell ya: it was a *weird* month.

I went to house parties until 4 a.m. with people I'd just met.

I went to a poetry reading I did not care about.

And I went on dates I would have normally skipped.

But I made friends that I'm still close to today, years later. Now, don't get me wrong: it wasn't all cake and ice cream. I had a ton of fear and resistance to most of those invitations. I didn't want to go camping when two new friends invited me, and I didn't want to go salsa dancing when a couple I just met told me to join them. I looked for every excuse in the book to back out of almost everything.

I'll say no just this once—nobody will know the difference.

I don't have the money to go camping.

I don't want to go salsa dancing; I will look like an idiot in front of lots of people.

I made an absolute fool of myself more times than I can count (salsa dancing went exactly as I had anticipated). And I spent a ton of money that I really didn't have that month.

But every single thing I said yes to turned out better than expected, without fail. Even events where I embarrassed myself felt like wins. I felt pride that I did something even though I didn't want to or have to.

THE 30-DAY SAY YES CHALLENGE

I dare you to try the 30-Day Say Yes Challenge. Here are the parameters:

- **Set a budget**—one of the biggest resistances to the Say Yes Challenge is the financial investment. Even though the relationships I built were hundreds of times more valuable than whatever I paid for drinks, meals, entrance fees, etc., it's a valid hesitation, especially if money's tight. You overcome that by creating a Say Yes budget that works for you. If you can only afford $10 for the month, then allot $10. If you can swing $100, then do it. Either way, keep track of how much you spend. If an invite *requires* you to spend money (such as a movie theatre ticket) *and* that money's not in your budget, then you get to say no. However, if someone invites you out to a "money optional" event or meet-up (such as drinks or dinner), you have to say yes, even if you just nurse a glass of water all night.

- **Say yes to every invitation**—the only caveat here is don't do anything that puts you in danger, like going into strange alleyways just because a "new friend" asked you to.

- **Do it for 30 days**—the Say Yes Challenge is not a long-term solution to make new friends. It's a kickstart. It's a restart. It's like taking a cold shower to boost your immune system. You don't want to *live* in a cold shower—you just hop in to get everything going again. That's like the Say Yes Challenge: it's not a long-term social strategy, mostly because you have to eventually find which people, events, and hobbies fit you best, rather than just letting the whims of the people around you dictate your whole life. A month is the perfect amount of time for the challenge.

- **Track it**—the best way to recognize your progress is to track it. Keep it simple: after every event, write it down in a spreadsheet or on a piece of paper. Over the course of the month, you'll feel a sense of pride at the growing list of events. It's like weightlifting: without tracking it, you're almost guaranteed to overlook your progress.

- **Bonus rule**—keep track of everyone you meet. If you write down these three pieces of information for every person you come across, you'll be shocked at how your social value will go through the roof:
  - The person's name
  - How you met them/where they live
  - A quick description of them

If you follow all of these rules for the Say Yes Challenge, I guarantee you that you'll end the month happier, more fulfilled, and with a much larger group of friends than when you started. And remember: don't beat yourself up if you say no to one invite. Shit happens. A single yes can make up for 10 noes.

Now that we've covered the big picture, let's go over some of the day-to-day tips that will help cultivate new friendships and how you can foster those relationships over time.

How to Make a Friend: A Template

Here are a few easy conversation pointers for the next time you meet someone.

INTRODUCE YOURSELF AND REMEMBER THEIR NAME

I am usually terrible at remembering names. I get so preoccupied with everything else going on, like figuring out how we are doing the greeting and keeping the conversation going, that five minutes in I'm trying to remember what they said their name was instead of listening to what they are currently saying.

Dominique? Larry? Shakira? Damn it.

In *Moonwalking with Einstein*, Joshua Foer who was the 2006 USA Memory Champion describes an easy way to remember any name or place.

"Create lavish images on the fly, to paint in the mind a scene so unlike any other it cannot be forgotten."

I used this trick to reduce my utter disgrace at my inability to remember who the hell was standing across from me multiple times. One particular incident involved the fiancé of one of my best friends. I had recently learned this slick maneuver and put it to the test.

Her parents, who I met briefly, introduced themselves as Leslie and Wayne. Immediately I put my brain to work and searched for an image, a movie to play in my mind that was something that "cannot be forgotten."

The first things that came to me for both of their names were as random as they were strange: Leslie's Pool Supplies is a national company I have seen on street corners since I was a kid. Check. And Wayne conjured up the Mike Meyers' movie *Wayne's World*.

So now there they were. Her astute and polite father rocking out to a guitar on an inflatable lounge chair in the middle of the pool as Leslie sunbathed herself. Their names have stuck with me ever since.

KEEP YOUR FIRST COMMENT OR QUESTION OPEN-ENDED

You have quite a few options after introductions, which can make it even more overwhelming. No matter what route you go, keep things open-ended. That way, you're not just asking a yes-or-no question that leads nowhere—you let the other person open up and show you a bit about themselves.

"How do you know [X person]?"

"Why did you decide to come here tonight?"

This is a no-brainer conversation starter, especially if you're at a party. Asking your new friend how they know the host, for example, makes them feel more comfortable. They have a chance to talk about why they're at the social event and who else they know there. It also gives you a lot of clues as to whether you're already in the same social circle as this new person or if you're truly complete strangers who just happen to know one mutual person.

Inevitably, they'll return the question, and you can tell them how you know your mutual acquaintance.

PARTY CONVERSATION PRO TIP

Stop for exactly one minute before you walk into any event/party. Use those 60 seconds to articulate to yourself how you know the host. That way, when you find yourself in this conversation, you'll be able to explain your relationship with the person in the most interesting way possible.

Also do this for events where you don't know anybody. If you explicitly state to yourself what interests you about the event, you'll be able to authentically explain it to anyone you meet.

If you make one friend after that, your 60 seconds of preparation can pay off in ways you can't imagine.

Alternatively, if you're meeting a group of two or more people for the first time, a can't-miss conversation starter is:

"How do you know each other?"

You'll usually see a glimmer of excitement in people's eyes when you ask this. They'll look at each other and reminisce, glad for the opportunity to relive how they met each other. They may have never thought about it since it happened, so you're giving them a gift to relive it.

If you're talking to a couple, just make a subtle shift in word choice:

"How did you two meet?"

MAKE A STATEMENT OR OBSERVATION

Let's assume you're talking to someone with decent social skills. That means they answered your open-ended question, and likely turned it back to you in some way. One of two things happens now:

1. Your first open-ended question led to a naturally flowing conversation.

2. Your first open-ended question led to a momentary dead end.

In the first case, congratulations—just let the conversation flow wherever it wants to go.

In the second scenario, you can respond with a statement or observation. I've found that if you ask someone a question (*"How do you know X person?"*) then jump into another question, it can feel a bit like a job interview. That's why I like to follow up a question with a statement.

Statements are a fun way to be playful with people and show a bit of your personality and interests. For example, if the person is drinking an IPA beer:

"You know, I used to only drink Coors Light, but those IPAs are starting to grow on me."

If you're talking to someone after a speaking event:

"When the keynote speaker opened up about her past— god, that was incredible."

These statements are a much more subtle way to open the door for other people's conversational participation without feeling like they're getting grilled.

Alternatively, you can go with the statement-question combo. I love this because it's more explicit about giving the other person information about me, while also asking something about them.

For example, if you're talking to someone at a park:

"It is beautiful here right now, reminds me of back home. What do you like to do outside this time of year?"

If you're talking to someone at a concert:

"That song reminded me of the time I took a road trip down to the Mexico border. Have you ever done that?"

EXIT GRACEFULLY

Knowing when to leave a conversation is a very underrated talent. It causes as much anxiety as knowing how to start and continue a conversation. But I've discovered a tactful, comfortable way to exit a conversation that I learned from watching the way a wiser friend did it.

Put out your hand for a handshake/fist or elbow bump and say:

"It's been great talking to you, [Name]. I'm gonna make the rounds, but I'm sure I'll run into you later on."

There's no need to make it awkward with some lie or excuse. If you have to go to the bathroom or grab another drink, tell them:

"I'm gonna run to the restroom/grab another drink and make the rounds, but I'm sure I'll see you in a bit."

If you don't have to go to the bathroom or grab another drink, just say you're going to make some rounds and you hope to see them again. Simple. Real. Comfortable. Anyone with any social tact will know that you're making a graceful exit, and they'll be grateful for it.

And someone without any social tact won't know the difference, so you're good either way.

GRAB CONTACT INFO

This step is the easiest to overlook. It's also the most important. It doesn't do much good to meet a potential friend then never see them again because you forgot to grab their phone number or email.

Whenever you're about to leave the event—whether it's a party, concert, convention, or rodeo—go back to the people you connected with and grab their contact info.

> Remember: everyone's a friend until proven otherwise.

SHOW UP AND FOLLOW UP

If you take only one concept away from this chapter let it be this:

You meet somebody new at a party, an orgy, at the library, or for coffee. You feel proud of yourself, and for good reason.

Now it's time to continue the momentum. The people I know with the best and most fulfilling relationships do two things better than anyone else:

They show up and they follow up.

That means after you connect with someone, you should continue to connect with them. Show up for other events they invite you to, and follow up by checking in on your new friends.

These are the little things that 98.5 percent of people don't do. They're all simple, easy to perform, and put you in the top 1.5 percent. Most people won't get the life they want because they won't do these annoying—yet utterly positive things. This social capital will compound over time and foster new areas for growth, more money, more freedom, and more enjoyment from existence.

- **Make the first move**—it's easy to think you can make a bunch of friends and social opportunities are going to come to you. You think, "If people really cared about me, they'd hit me up." Get that thought out of your head. Everyone is busy, just like you, and everyone is waiting for someone else to make the first move. Be that person who reaches out when everyone else is scared of looking "desperate." Any of the following thoughts are a sign you should text someone:

- "I haven't talked to Sarah in a while."
- "I wonder what Pete's been doing lately."
- "Did Justin move to Chicago?"
- "This ice cream cone/movie/meme reminds me of them."

- **Call on their birthday**—at the beginning of every month, I check Facebook to see whose birthdays are coming up that month. Then I put those birthdays in my planner and call each person on their big day. This is way more personal and appreciated than a Facebook post that says "hbd" or even a text message.

- **Keep track of where they live**—I'm not saying you should ask someone you just met what their address is. If you do that, they'll expect to see you lurking on their street in a white van at 2 a.m. Instead, here's what I do: every time I put someone's name and number in my phone, I add a note with their home city. That way when someone I know needs a connection in a certain city, I can just search that city in my contacts and connect them. My new friend Sarah is moving to Denver? I search "Denver" in my contacts and hook Sarah up with my other friends there. Someone else needs a car in Sacramento? I search my contacts again and see if any Sacramento folks have a beater for sale. It's simple to add someone's city to their contact in your phone, but the results are incredible. You become the person everyone goes to when they need a hookup in a new city and you can easily connect with people when you visit a new place. That's powerful.

- **Share your shit first**—too many people just show each other the good shit in their lives. The new car, the new apartment, a grand vacation. You can't connect with someone without sharing the shit in your lives. As Robert Glover famously said, we are "attracted to each other's rough edges." And nobody wants to share their shit first. So be a leader and break the ice by sharing something you're insecure about. Even on a date, there's no better way to quickly connect than by telling the pretty girl sitting across the table that you're feeling nervous. That brings humanity to the interaction, instead of it feeling like an interview.

Little actions, the ones nobody really notices in the moment, those are the ones that build incredible relationships *over time*. Got a birthday dinner you promised to go to, but the night comes and you're too tired? I've been there 100 times. Most people would bail. Don't be most people. Go anyway. It's always worth it. Did you see somebody for the first time in a while and it felt great? Shoot them a text the next day and say that.

Relationships take effort to build, but if you show up and follow up, you'll be well on your way to building a large, fulfilling social circle and life.

Life, Love, and Relationships Are Not Certain

It was an unusually warm day for that time of year, with a bright blue sky and crisp air as we walked past colorful bay houses to his favorite coffee shop.

I met one of my best friends, Bradley, in high school when we sat down next to each other in the training room at the hardware store where we had both been hired. He eventually went on to become a firefighter with the city of San Francisco. I've always admired him because he's damn good at his job. He's decisive, he never seems to get stressed, even in life-or-death scenarios, and he follows his instincts.

But on this beautiful winter day as we caught up on our lives, I noticed something different about him. He was still the same dude I admired—still funny, still cool, still easy-going—but something had changed in him. Something good. Almost like he'd gained a depth that I couldn't put my finger on.

I asked him about it.

"Shit man, I saw something last week that changed me." He took a sip of his coffee. "Got a call in the middle of a weekday. Pleasant afternoon like today. A lady leaves her yoga class and she's on the street putting her equipment in the trunk of her car. Just as she was doing that, a driver coming up the street was texting and driving. He got distracted, swerved into the parking lane, and crushed the woman with his car. She's dead, just like that. She didn't do anything wrong, but in an instant it didn't matter."

A smiling couple strolled past us on the sidewalk and gave us a nod. We smiled back.

"That must have impacted you," I said.

He nodded, then said something that has stuck with me ever since.

"I've seen quite a few dead people since I came out here. When you see death like that—as an everyday occurrence—it forces you to constantly reevaluate your life and your priorities. You can do everything right and still lose your life. There's no guarantee of anything. If your number gets called, it's called."

Freeze frame. It's one moment before that car crashes into the woman on the street in San Francisco. No trolley bells, no bustling foot traffic, no seagulls squawking—just silence and stillness.

Imagine yourself in her shoes, frozen in time before you meet your demise.

What do you think about?

What will you miss?

What do you wish you'd done?

Maybe you'll wish you'd spent more time working. Maybe you'll think you should have held that grudge longer. Or maybe you'll miss the hours of YouTube videos you watched.

Not likely.

You'll regret the risks you *didn't* take, the things you *didn't* say, and you'll miss the people you know you'll never see again.

In other words, if you have the luxury of retrospection on your deathbed, your final thoughts will be on your relationships—both with other people, and with yourself.

Your priorities may shift over time. Maybe you switch from yoga to kickboxing, or change jobs and cities. Maybe you switch the early mornings for late nights. Either way, your relationships define your life. And the more time you spend fostering those relationships, the more fulfilling your life will be.

Unfortunately, nobody tells you when your number will get called. As moments pass by, nobody tells us that this is it. That woman with the yoga equipment didn't get a freeze frame moment and neither will you.

We won't be sitting in our grandma's backyard enjoying a barbecue, and see big flashing letters in the sky saying, "This Is the Last Barbecue Your Grandma Will Ever Have!"

You won't be dancing at your friend's going away party and feel the buzz of a text message that says, "You will never see any of these people again."

You'll never read a tweet that says, "You'll only see your parents for three more Christmases."

We don't get that luxury. Those things just happen, usually without a word of warning. Life is made up of small moments. It takes only one of those moments for someone's life to end, but it also takes a single moment to send a text message. To call someone you've lost touch with. To say hello to someone new and invite them into your life.

It's easy to get stuck in the details of our lives, unable to see through the mass of green tangles like the jungle of the Darien Gap. We get caught up in details—like the asshole who cut us off in traffic, a snarky comment our sibling made, or our dwindling checking account.

But no matter how important those things feel right now, those worries will end one day, and every person you love will eventually die. Will you live each day assuming you'll see them again, or will you work hard to get closer to the people you love, knowing that nothing in this life is a given—even the next moment?

CHAPTER 5

Live Like Nobody's Watching

"So let's go out with a bang...remember, they're just jokes. We're all gonna die soon and there's no sequel."

——**Ricky Gervais**

I'm sure you've seen the phrase online:

"Dance like nobody's watching."

It's a valid enough sentiment: the idea is that you should move across the dancefloor with no worries about what other people think of you. Instead, you dance the way you want to, and move through the world with your desires leading the beat, not other people's perceptions of you.

What if, instead of just dancing that way, you could live your whole life that way?

What if you could live like nobody would ever find out what you did?

No, I don't mean you should disregard all social norms and live off the grid (although I know plenty of happy people who have done that).

I'm talking about living life on your own terms, and rewriting the rules to fit your values, needs, and dreams.

Throughout the book we've talked a lot about how to improve your lot in life: how to grow a stronger community, how to shake off the patterns and habits of the past and the ways to build a life worth the struggle. Those are all valid and healthy pursuits, and I think you should work your ass off to get them.

But in this chapter, I want to talk about what comes

after you reach those goals. What do you do if you get the friends you've always wanted, the life you need, and you still feel like something's missing?

Reaching your goals is extremely gratifying, but it also creates a huge problem…

What's next?

The Next Shiny Thing

NOTES FROM THE STUDIO:
FREEDOM IS NOT EXTERNAL

"We're all chasing a sense of purpose, which is great, but we've all been misled to believe that sense of purpose can come through our jobs and money. It just doesn't always work that way.

"You try to accrue money because you think money will give you the freedom to finally live your purpose. That may be true to a certain extent, but money will never make you feel complete in and of itself.

"If you find your purpose and live it every day, I promise it won't matter how big your house is or how nice your car is, because no thing can change the completeness you feel from living your purpose.

"And so, if we can work—as individuals—on feeling

Life can feel like a straight line, bringing you from one activity to the next, constantly looking on the horizon for the next best thing. The truth is, no matter what you accomplish or how much you achieve, if you don't find peace and fulfillment in yourself, you'll *never* get it from someone or somewhere else.

No matter how much you accomplish.

The Eldrick Dilemma

In 1995, an amateur golfer by the name of Eldrick tied for 41st place in the Masters Tournament. Aside from being the only amateur in the tournament, there was something else notable about Eldrick: he was only 19 years old.

Two years later, he came back and *won* the Masters. At 21, he was the youngest winner in tournament history, and he was the first African American to ever win the Masters.

Eventually, Eldrick won more than 80 PGA Tour events, and cemented himself as one of the best golfers of all time.

By the early 2000s, the entire world knew Eldrick, but they called him by a different name: Tiger Woods.

In 2009, the world had a few new names for him: liar, adulterer, and womanizer.

More than a dozen women came forward—everyone from cocktail waitresses to porn stars—claiming they'd had affairs with Tiger Woods while he was married to his wife, who was a Swedish model. The squeaky-clean brand Tiger had painstakingly created over the years was suddenly ruined.

In 2010, in his first interview after a self-imposed exile, he put it best:

"I tried to stop, and I couldn't stop. It was just—it was horrific."

He then continued to drop this:

"Stripping away denial and rationalization, you start coming to the truth of who you really are, and that can be very ugly. But then again, when you face it and you start conquering it and you start living up to it, the strength that I feel now—I've never felt that kind of strength."

After his public fallout at the pinnacle of his career, Tiger disappeared from the limelight. The media circus died down, his wife left him, and the parade of porn stars left town. Tiger retreated into his own world to handle the grave mistakes he'd made.

In 2011, he fell from number 1 in the world golf rankings to number 58.

In 2013, he returned to his number 1 ranking, and led the PGA Tour in money winnings.

Back surgeries hobbled him after that, causing him to compete in only one tournament between August 2015 and January 2018, and he fell off the list of the world's top 1,000 golfers.

His career was done. He was a shadow of his former self. Then, in 2019, a comeback.

A full decade after his scandal, and more than 11 years after his last major tournament victory, Tiger the 43-year-old won the Masters—the same tournament that had cemented his celebrity in the golf world when he was just 21 years old.

On the surface, Tiger Woods had everything anyone could ever want. The man was the best in the world at what he did, he had earned more than a billion dollars from golfing and endorsements, and he was married to a Swedish model.

But that wasn't good enough for him.

Because nothing could be enough for anybody who seeks fulfillment from outside sources.

I'm not knocking achievement or marrying Swedish models—quite the contrary. I think those are noble, admirable pursuits. I'm just saying that Tiger Woods had a hole inside of him that he was trying to fill with outside stuff.

We desperately piece together the parts of our life to "have it all together." Our attention needs attention. We need to improve our self-improvement for the sake of improvement. Develop your damn development.

That outside stuff—achievement, sex, money, the "perfect" life—shouldn't be the things we seek to find balance. They should be a supplement to the internal balance we already have.

And even when things have become unbalanced to the point of Tiger, it's never too late to find it again. We can always make a comeback.

You Are the Best the World Has Ever Seen

So what's the problem? Why do anything? Why don't we live relaxing on the couch all day stuffing our faces with burgers, Oreos, and mindless entertainment?

Part of the problem is that we do have the best in the world. Through podcasts and social media, we have more access to celebrities and their personal lives than ever. Through Netflix and Hulu, we have more access to the best media and entertainment ever created.

It's hard not to compare ourselves with the top performers in the world, so taking what we have for granted seems like a given. We lose sight of the journey we're on and instead focus on what's ahead instead of what is right in front of our face.

NOTES FROM THE STUDIO:
PROCESS OVER GOALS

Larry Yatch is a leadership expert who uses his experience as a Navy SEAL to train people in business. He had this to say about focusing on process over achievement:

"I was what you might call a 'high performer' in high school. College, too. In fact, all throughout life—even in my professional life—I derived a sense of my identity from working harder, doing better, and achieving more. Even if it meant suffering. That mentality was deeply ingrained in me: you have to suffer to reach your goals.

"Eventually, I realized that I had it backwards. My hyper-focus on the goal led to my suffering. On the other hand, hyper-focus on the process led to happiness as well as reaching the goal.

"The example I like to use is the 70-year-old lady who has

> a booth at a flea market I go to. She makes jewelry out of garbage that she finds, then sells it at the flea market. She's one of the happiest people I've ever met. She can't wait to wake up each morning to look for garbage. Because to her, it isn't garbage—it's something to turn beautiful, and an excuse to talk to nice people at the flea market all day.
>
> "Plenty of people would look at her and say she doesn't have much. That she's a loser with no higher ambition. But she wins every single day, because she makes the process her goal, rather than seeking some performance marker.
>
> "I've put a lot of effort into changing my philosophy to match hers. Rather than seeking high performance, I seek perfection in my daily practice—then let my goals come naturally."

Process over goals is a badass philosophy. So I turn it around to you: could you live your life for the simple joy of doing, and nothing else?

Would you be satisfied if you did great things with your life, *but nobody found out?*

Only you can answer that question. To be perfectly honest, I don't know if I could do that—otherwise you wouldn't be reading this book. You have to look within yourself and see if you're really focused on the things that matter or if you're just chasing for the sake of it.

CONCLUSION

The Fire of Heaven

"If given the chance to turn back, I would not take it. Therefore, the decision to go ahead is my own responsibility, to be accepted with a whole heart."

—Peter Matthiessen, *The Snow Leopard*

It was my last season as a wildland firefighter, and our crew was on assignment in a remote part of Idaho, two hours from the nearest town. Sure, it was September, but in the Rocky Mountains, early September can be the dead of winter.

That's exactly what the freak snowstorm intended to

remind us of. But we had no idea. Our only contact with the outside world was updates on the fire from a nearby station. Nothing about the weather forecast.

Our mission was simple: we were on mop up duty, which meant the local fire crews had contained the main fire, and we were just making sure it didn't burn past its perimeters.

I wasn't a rookie anymore. I was a grizzled vet, with the tobacco-can imprint in my pants and the two-week stubble to prove it. I loved firefighting, but I struggled to see a future for myself out there in the woods. My gut told me it was time for something new. A blizzard wasn't what I had in mind.

We made camp on the last night of the assignment. The air was cool, but comfortable. We had gathered the dead, charred wood from the blaze to make a bonfire. We proceeded to sit around laughing and talking into the night like we always did.

When it was time for bed, I climbed into my sleeping bag wearing light sweatpants and a T-shirt. Over the course of the night, the temperatures dropped. Then dropped some more. I could barely sleep wondering what the hell was happening. Snow started to fall, and my teeth chattered as I drifted closer to hypothermia. I could have gotten up and grabbed some heavier clothes, or asked someone else to loan me a jacket, but I couldn't fathom moving or talking, even if staying still meant I'd freeze to death.

When the first light of morning engulfed the forest, I saw that six inches of snow had fallen that September night. I shook myself out of my sleeping bag like a sled dog before a race, and we got another fire going, made once again out of the dead wood of the forest.

The warm crackling fire emitted its yellow warmth, and I huddled next to it with my crew. That fire felt like heaven. And it was in that moment that I realized I was done with firefighting. It had given me a lot over the four years I did it: it gave me a mission without going into a 9-5 job, a chance to learn how to lead and feel useful, and it got me out of my parents' house. But its time had passed. Now, I couldn't fathom another day frozen in place, even if that place was heaven.

I had to let go of who I was so I could move on to something better.

Let Go of Who You Are

There's an old fable that instructs us how to hold onto something. It says that if you put your hand out, palms down, you have to clench what you desire. If you don't clench, whatever object you're holding will fall to the ground the moment you relax your grip.

If you held your hand like this, you might think you have to clench the rest of your life for fear of losing what you desire. But the fable hints at a better way:

By simply turning your palm to the sky and releasing your grip on the object of your desire, you take away the stress of your clench. Of course, the object may fall off your hand, but it also has the chance to remain. Not because you're forcing it to, but because the laws of the universe keep it in place.

In the same way, we have to let go of who we think we are. Who we want others to see us as. Let go of what we thought life was going to look like at this age and the patterns that are in our head, creating the same situations over and over again. Let go of who you used to be. Let go, even, of the person you're trying to become.

Move forward without expectations, with an open

mind and an open heart, and you'll be shocked at where you end up.

But no matter how low your life gets, you can always make a comeback. You can let go of the patterns that no longer serve you, and have turned you to the same vices repeatedly. And once you stop clutching to who you were then and who you are now, you can finally allow yourself to become who you were always meant to be.

"There isn't going to be a turning point...There isn't going to be any next-month-it'll-be-better, next fucking year, next fucking life. You don't have any time to wait for. You just got to look around you and say: So this is it. This is really all there is to it... Everybody just needing such little things and they can't get them. Everybody needing just a little...confidence from somebody else... Everybody, you know, reaching out tentatively but drawing back...it seems like such a shame. It's so close to being really right and good and open."

—Janis Joplin

Resources

Hey there. It's me, at the end of the book. If you want to read a bit more, get a bonus chapter at alexstarr.com/bonuschapter.

To see the Rewrite the Rules store, join the community, get a cool weekly email and more, head to alexstarr.com.

You can also follow me on IG @alexhstarr and can find *Rewrite the Rules with Alex Starr* on any podcast platform.

I deeply appreciate you reading this book. If you got something out of it, if it changed your perspective or helped you in any way...I ask that you help pay it forward to a friend or family member you think would benefit from reading it. We need more people taking that bold step into a new place.

- Alex

Books Referenced

- *The War of Art* by Steven Pressfield
- *You Are Here* by Thich Nhat Hanh
- *Man's Search for Meaning* by Victor Frankl
- *The Fifth Sacred Thing* by Starhawk
- *Tribe: On Homecoming and Belonging* by Sebastian Junger
- *Zen and the Art of Motorcycle Maintenance* by Robert Pirsig
- *The Snow Leopard* by Peter Matthiessen

Contact Info For Podcasts
Mentioned In The Book

⚒ *Donald Hoffman*, Episodes 32 & 33
- ○ 🐦 donalddhoffman
- ○ TED Talk: "Do we see reality as it is?"

⚒ *Alonso Hernandez*, Episode 9

⚒ *Laith*, Episode 69
- ○ 📷 oklaith

⚒ *Erick Godsey*, Episode 77
- ○ 📷 erickgodsey
- ○ Erickgodsey.com

⚒ *Manuela and Sam*, Episode 63
- ○ 📷 expeditionkindness

⚒ *Yes Theory*, Episode 14
- ○ 📷 yestheory
- ○ Yestheory.com

⚒ *Kyle Holsinger*, Episode 2

⚒ *Rob Greenfield*, Episode 44
- ○ 📷 robjgreenfield
- ○ Robgreenfield.org

⚒ *Larry Yatch*, Episodes 40 & 41
- ○ 📘 sealteamleaders
- ○ Sealteamleaders.com

Recommended Social Media Accounts to Follow

- ⚒ ⊙ thinkgrowprosper
- ⚒ ⊙ __nitch
- ⚒ ⊙ davidgoggins
- ⚒ ⊙ outlawpoets
- ⚒ ⊙ humansofny
- ⚒ ⊙ andyfrisella
- ⚒ 🐦 naval
- ⚒ ⊙ jannabreslin

- ⚒ 🐦 kamalravikant
- ⚒ ⊙ jesseitzler
- ⚒ ◪ realtimcannon
- ⚒ ⊙ jesse.sussman
- ⚒ ⊙ ramit
- ⚒ ⊙ heart_of_travel
- ⚒ ⊙ queenconnector

Acknowledgments

As the famous naturalist John Muir proclaimed, "when we try to pick out anything by itself, we find it hitched to everything else in the universe."

Nothing could be closer to the truth when trying to express pieces of gratitude for a project such as this, for where is the appropriate place to begin? Do I thank my mom's OBGYN?

I will proceed here from the heart first and my brain second as best I can.

Firstly, to my beautiful fiancé Ashley. When we first met, neither one of us knew how to be in a regular relationship and now we are on our way to being in a married relationship. You make waking up in the morning something to be grateful for. Thank you for making me dinner even when I was frustrated and being difficult, giving incredible advice on drafts of the book and making me Oreo shakes when something sweet was needed. Your never-ending support could keep me alive forever. I love you.

A big ol' shoutout to my close friend and editor Greg Larson. I handed you a giant and disjointed mess and you helped craft an actual book. Your guidance is literally the only reason this book is now in people's hands and I am forever grateful. Thanks for helping me through the emotional rollercoaster on countless calls, being honest, meeting up for frisbee hangs, and being a true friend.

Jesse Sussman, you are a genius at book launches and have been there for laughs and knowledge throughout this entire process as a friend and source of inspiration. I appreciate everything you have done and continue to do, including coming over for insightful dinners and eating all of our food.

Cindy Curtis, I want to thank you for bringing this to

life. Your professionalism, artistic talent and patience made all the difference to me and the readers. Can't wait to work with you again in the near future.

Dad, you were the first person who planted the seed in my young mind that I could do something after college that wasn't a standard job and to this day I am still waiting to hear you complain about anything. Thanks for showing me how to be a man in the world today and letting me find my own way. Mom, you have always been there as somebody I could turn to under any circumstance. Thanks for showing me how to treat people and socialize, being a sounding board on endless phone conversations, and constantly helping in any way you could with the book. Carly and Maddy, you both are the best sisters a guy could ask for. Thanks for your constant support and showing me what sibling love looks like.

To everyone who was on the AmeriCorps Water 6 team: we slept in the basement of a church together and hiked remote mountains while becoming a family in a short amount of time and those experiences with you are still some of the fondest memories of my life. Thanks for being there during all of it and being true friends I could count on.

US Forest Service Crew 5, y'all are brothers (and a sister) to me and each of you have shaped the way I look at my life forever. Thanks for watching my back, sharing countless jokes, and being people I could always rely on whether we were stuck in a lightning storm or trying to find an appropriate place to water down.

Booster and Boonie: thanks for giving me food when I would forget lunch, laughing our way through road trips, and keeping me company trying to find ways to not work. You guys are the reason I stayed down there on the border for so long.

Kyle Holsinger, we did one of my first podcasts together with the microphones on a dirty box on a dusty porch. Your story inspired me to begin all of this. Thanks for never saying no to a drink at the saloon and explaining how hockey works.

Kevin, thanks for being honest about your experiences and letting me share them here. Your growing family is lucky to have you as a husband and dad.

Every guest I have had on the podcast and shared their truth and story to the world: thanks for taking the time and being a part of something special.

To the rest of my friends and family who have always been supportive of my endeavors, you have impacted me and I appreciate you more than you can imagine. I love you all.

About the Author

ALEX STARR had questions around the next stage of life after graduating college so he decided to join a domestic version of the Peace Corps where he completed 1700 hours of service and earned the bronze Congressional Medal of Service.

From there he became a Wildland Firefighter on an Initial Attack Crew for multiple seasons to battle some of the west's largest blazes from California to Alaska.

Throughout his travels in the US and South America, he started the top-rated "Rewrite the Rules" podcast which showcases alternative lifestyles and unique stories from around the world. Some of his guests include best-selling authors, former gang members, Navy SEALs, polyamourous lovers, CEO's, people living out of a van, billionaires, and cognitive scientists.

The show has now been downloaded over 100,000 times in over 30 countries.

He has been lost in the desert on horseback, ripped the head off a chicken after being pressured by an 80 year-old grandma, and occasionally seeks validation from strangers.

He now lives in Austin, TX with his fiance Ashley and their tiny, yet fierce dog Macy.

To join the community and read new content, visit alexstarr.com or follow Alex on Instagram at @alexhstarr.

You can find *Rewrite the Rules with Alex Starr,* on any podcast platform.

Made in the USA
Monee, IL
30 April 2021